Time for MENTALS

Paul Nightingale

6

Book 6

HUNTER
EDUCATION
NIGHTINGALE

Copyright © 2015 Paul Nightingale
Time for Mentals - Book 6

Published by:
Hunter Education Nightingale
ABN: 69 055 798 626
PO Box 547
Warners Bay NSW 2282
Ph: 0417 658 777
email: sales@huntereducationnightingale.com.au
        paul@huntereducationnightingale.com.au
        www.huntereducationnightingale.com.au

Cover Design: Brooke Lewis

National Library of Australia Card No.
and ISBN 978 - 1 - 922242 - 15 - 0

RECYCLING

When the program is completed and the paper no longer wanted, be sure to have it recycled. The time and care taken to recycle may help save a tree and maintain our environment.

E	D	C	B	A
19	18	17	16	15

ime for Mentals
ook 6

out this Book

ie for Mentals - Year 6 is the last in a series
seven books that addresses the Year 6 Level
scriptions and sections of the new Mathematics
riculum. This book reinforces the concept and
ivities introduced in the strands found in its
fect partner Time for Maths - Year 6. The book
n also be used for homework or extension.

en this book is used in parallel with Time for
ths - Year 6, a solid meaningful understanding
Number and Place Value, Patterns and Algebra,
ng Units of Measurement along with interpreting
d representing data will be achieved by the
ld. In addition the child will learn the language
mathematics so the processes and concepts
come more enriching as he/she moves from unit
unit.

Time for Mentals -
Year 6 contains 28 self
contained units, each of four sections. Answers
to all activities are provided at the end of the
book for the teacher or parent. This support
and knowledge will help the child develop
understanding and build confidence with
mathematics.

While the book is a valuable extension,
reinforcement and builder of mathematics skills in
the classroom, it is also an ideal learning tool for
use at home.

Message to Parents

A child using Time for Mentals - Year 6 helps develop an understanding of mathematical
concepts - a parent should resist the temptation to actually provide answers but support
and assist when necessary.

As a parent you help your child learn everyday. This book provides activities to help develop
concepts, processes and proficiencies needed for the development of mathematics, which
parents can assist with as the child moves from unit to unit.

At all times encourage and praise each units performance by the child. Help by checking
answers, but remember the understanding of mathematical concepts develop over time
with practice.

Enjoy, encourage and praise your child's work at home as he/she moves towards mastering the
proficiencies and understanding of mathematics. This book provides activities to enable parents
to help develop the child's concepts, processes and skills.

Place Value

1. Write the number showing on each abacus.

   a.

   M HTH TTH TH H T O

   _____

   b.

   M HTH TTH TH H T O

   _____

2. Write millions, hundred thousands, ten thousands, thousands, hundreds, tens or ones according to place value for the circled numbers.

   a. 4 6③7 2 1 8   _____

   b. 6 7 8 3⑤1 9   _____

   c. 2④0 3 0 1 7   _____

   d. 6 8 4 1 9 3⑧   _____

   e. ③3 3 4 8 2 1   _____

3. Write the number 150 more than each of these.

   a. 6 253 854   _____

   b. 7 443 667   _____

   c. 8 135 026   _____

   d. 3 300 502   _____

4. Round off each number to the **nearest** million.

   a. 6 362 143   _____

   b. 65 721 611   _____

   c. 4 441 213   _____

   d. 1 631 214   _____

5. Write the number 1500 **less** than each of these.

   a. 7 241 366   _____

   b. 2 467 524   _____

   c. 3 321 645   _____

   d. 4 175 150   _____

Addition

1. Add these numbers.

   a. 5 million + 8 hundred thousand + 6 thousand + 4 hundred and 10

   _____

   b. 4 hundred thousand + 7 thousand + 5 hundred + 6 tens + 8 ones.

   _____

   c. 8 million + 7 thousand + 9 hundred + 5 tens + 6 ones.

   _____

2. Using addition strategies, find the sum of numbers in the ovals.

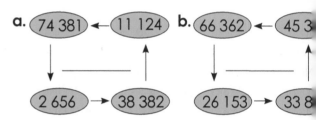

   a. 74 381 ← 11 124   **b.** 66 362 ← 45 3

   2 656 → 38 382   26 153 → 33 8

3. **a.** 6 2 3 4 2
      1 5 7 7 8
   + 1 2 7 9 6
   _____

   b. 4 4 3 5 4
      8 6 4 6
   + 3 2 9 5 1
   _____

   c. 6 2 5 ⁛
      1 5 6 ⁛
   + 2 2 7 ⁛
   _____

4. Write the algorithm for the numbers and then write the total.

   74 362   71 592

   24 688   3 385

   +_____
   _____

5. Find the sum of money for each algorithm.

   a. $623.85
      147.72
   + 246.88
   _____

   b. $523.82
      436.75
   + 172.66
   _____

   c. $129.⁛
      258.⁛
   + 493.⁛
   _____

6. 47326 + 17538 + 26862 = ☐

4

Length

Write the unit of length for each object in metres (m) centimetres (cm) or millimetres (mm).

a.

b.

c.

22 ____   32 ____   38 ____

d.

e.

f.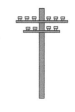

42 ____   10 ____   7 ____

Find the length of each line using a scale.
5mm = 4m

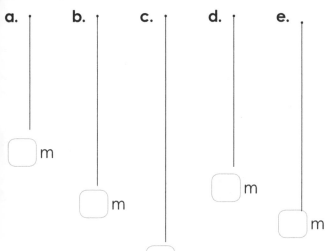

a. ☐ m

b. ☐ m

c. ☐ m

d. ☐ m

e. ☐ m

Complete the table and then complete the activities.

a. ____ mm = 1cm   **d.** 40mm = ____ cm

b. 100cm = ____ m   **e.** 4km = ____ m

c. ____ m = 1km   **f.** 500m = ____ km

Measure the length of each object in millimetres.

a. ____ mm

b. ____ mm

c. ____ mm

d.  ____ mm

e. ____ mm

f. ____ mm

Time

1. Make a personal timeline with the year each event happened in your life. Write the year.

Born	Kindy	Age 9	Year 3	Today
↓	↓	↓	↓	↓
____	____	____	____	____

2. Write each pm time in 24-hour time.

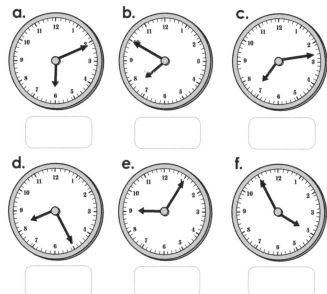

a. ☐   **b.** ☐   **c.** ☐

d. ☐   **e.** ☐   **f.** ☐

3. Add or subtract time showing on the pm clock face. Write the new time in 24-hour time.

a. Subtract 8 minutes   **b.** Add $1\frac{1}{2}$ hours

c. Add 24 minutes   **d.** Subtract 52 minutes

4. Write each analogue time in 24-hour time.

a. 7:30am _____   **b.** 4:50am _____

c. 11:20pm _____   **d.** 7:45pm _____

e. 12:13am _____   **f.** 8:52pm _____

5. Write each time in either am or pm time.

a. Quarter to midnight _____

b. Ten minutes to noon _____

c. Half past midnight _____

d. Thirty minutes after noon _____

5

Prime and Composite Numbers

1. Circle only the **prime numbers**.

   2   3   4   5   7   9   11   13

   17   19   21   23   29   31   35

2. Write the factors for each number.

   a. 8 ⬚ ⬚ ⬚ and ⬚

   b. 16 ⬚ ⬚ ⬚ ⬚ and ⬚

   c. 24 ⬚ ⬚ ⬚ ⬚ ⬚ ⬚ and ⬚

   d. 28 ⬚ ⬚ ⬚ ⬚ ⬚ and ⬚

3. How many prime numbers between zero and 20? ⬚

4. What is the sum of the prime numbers between zero and 20? ⬚

5. A set of consecutive primes, which have a difference of two, is called a set of twin primes. What are the first set of twin primes?

   _____ and _____

6. Complete each factor tree to find the prime factors of each number.

   a. 12
   2

   b. 16
   2

   c. 20
   5

7. Write the number with each of these prime factors.

   a. 2 x 2 x 3 x 5   b. 2 x 3 x 5 x 7   c. 2 x 3 x 3 x 5

   ⬚   ⬚   ⬚

Subtraction

1. Complete each subtraction algorithm.

a.	4517	b.	5468	c.	3879
	-1302		-2254		-1646

2. Trade ones, tens and hundreds to find the difference in these five-digit algorithms.

a.	62535	b.	24687
	-10456		-11599

c.	68544	d.	39567
	-12765		-14388

3. Complete the subtraction grid. Subtract the number on the side from the top number in each column.

—	3697	5838	6577
a. 1428			
b. 3155			
c. 2468			
d. 1279			

4. Find the difference between each sum of money.

a.	$276.58	b.	$458.73	c.	$389.5
	-$113.47		-$127.88		-$249.8

5. A farmer had 12 265 sheep to shear. If 7 388 were already shorn, how many were left to shear?

   _____

Length

Find the perimeter of each shape.
(Lengths are not to scale.)

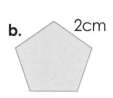 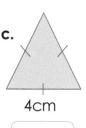 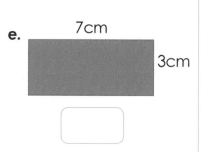

a. 4cm
m

b. 2cm

c.

4cm

d. 3cm e. 7cm

3cm

Write each length in decimal notation.

a. 4 kilometres 530 metres _____

b. 2 kilometres 750 metres _____

c. 10 kilometres 240 metres _____

d. 450 metres _____

e. 27 metres _____

Convert each length to an equivalent standard unit of measure.

a. 380 centimetres = _____ m

b. 7 250 metres = _____ km

c. 2 500 millimetres = _____ m

d. 6 280 centimetres = _____ km

e. 75 centimetres = _____ m

Measure the length of each line in millimetres.

a. _____ mm

b. _____ mm

c. _____ mm

Transformation

1. **Reflect**, **translate** or **rotate** these shapes.

a.  reflect

b.  rotate

c.  translate

d. rotate

2. Describe the transformation of each shape. Use **flip**, **slide** or **turn**.

a.

b.

c.

3. Colour the shapes you could use to make a tessellating pattern.

a. 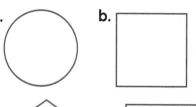 b. 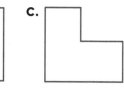 c.

d. 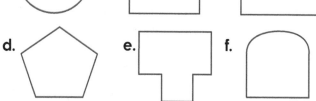 e. f.

4. Continue this pattern.

Rounding Off

1. Round off each number to the **nearest ten**.

   a. 657 _____   b. 842 _____

   c. 375 _____   d. 635 _____

   e. 721 _____   f. 547 _____

2. Round off each number to the **nearest hundred**.

   a. 657 _____   b. 842 _____

   c. 375 _____   d. 635 _____

   e. 721 _____   f. 547 _____

3. Round off each number to the **nearest thousand**.

   a. 4531 _____   b. 6275 _____

   c. 8131 _____   d. 6175 _____

   e. 7728 _____   f. 4981 _____

4. Draw a line from each number to the **nearest thousand** on the number line.

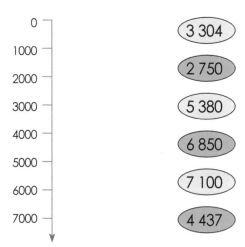

5. Use rounding off to find the approximate totals for each addition.

   a. 603 + 298 ≈ _____   b. 389 + 208 ≈ _____

   c. 392 + 497 ≈ _____   d. 203 + 496 ≈ _____

6. Round off both factors to the nearest 100 and 10 and then write an approximate product.

   a. 217 x 81 ≈ _____   b. 394 x 22 ≈ _____

Multiplication

1. Use the contracted method to complete each multiplication.

   a.   1 2 3 4
       x 3
      _____

      _____

   b.   1 8 1 4
       x 7
      _____

      _____

   c.   3 8 0
       x
      _____

      _____

   d. 2 4 6 8 2
       x 4
      _____

      _____

   e. 3 3 1 2 7
       x 6
      _____

      _____

   f. 1 6 5

      _____

      _____

2. Complete the multiplication web.

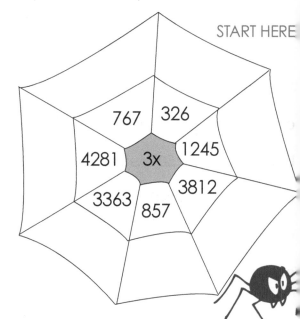

3. Find the product.

   a. 176 and 8 _____   b. 752 and 3 _____

   c. 2375 and 4 _____   d. 1765 and 5 _____

4. Use the contracted form to find the total sum of money in each algorithm.

   a. $ 2 6 . 6 3
      x 3
      _____

      _____

   b. $ 4 8 . 9 3
      x 5
      _____

      _____

   c. $ 4 3 .
      x
      _____

      _____

   d. $ 1 5 6 . 7 4
       x 3
      _____

      _____

   e. $ 7 5 8 . 4 5
       x 6
      _____

      _____

Mass

Write the unit of mass for each object in kg or T.

a.

b.

c.

85 _____   385 _____   600 _____

d.

e.

f.

48 _____   2 _____   2 _____

Write the mass showing on each scale in kilograms.

[ ] kg   [ ] kg   [ ] kg

Write each mass in its **shortest** form.

a. 4 000 grams _____   b. 500 grams _____

c. 750 grams _____   d. 9 500 grams _____

a. How many 100g are needed to balance 1 kilogram? [ ]

b. How many 50g are needed to balance 750 grams? [ ]

c. What is the mass of 500mL of water? [ ]

a. Paris' mass is 56 kilograms, which includes her school bag. If Paris is 52kg, what is the mass of her bag? [ ]

b. If 4 containers of water have a mass of 2.8kg, what is the mass of ten containers? [ ] kg

Graphs

1. Use the line graph to complete the questions.

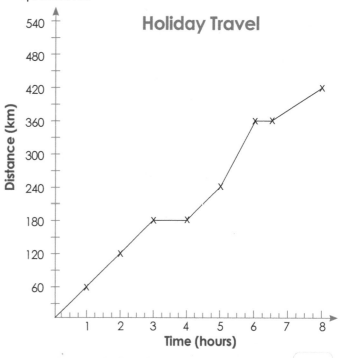

1. How long did it take to travel 180km? [ ]

2. What distance was travelled in 2 hours? [ ] km

3. How many rest periods are shown on the graph? [ ]

4. How long was the first rest? [ ]

5. What was the speed travelled in the first 3 hours? (*Hint: find distance and time*) [ ] km/h

6. How many kilometres were travelled between 4 and 5 hours? [ ] km

7. How long did it take to travel 420 km? (include rest time) [ ] hrs

8. If there were no rests, how long would the journey have taken? [ ] hrs

9. How many hours between the two rest breaks? [ ] hrs

10. What was the total time taken for the two rest periods? [ ] hrs

11. How long did it take to travel the last 60 kilometres? [ ] hrs

12. If the car travelled another 120 kilometres at 60 km/hour, how long would the trip take? [ ] hrs

9

Square Numbers

1. Write the square numbers shown by each of these groups.

a. 　b. 　c. 　d.

e. 　f.

2. Complete the table of square numbers.

6^2	10^2	5^2	8^2	11^2	9^2

3. Complete each number sentence.

a. $6^2 - 7 =$　b. $8^2 + 7 =$　c. $5^2 + 2^2 =$

d. $7^2 + 4^2 =$　e. $3^2 + 9^2 =$　f. $10^2 - 9^2 =$

g. $4^2 + 2^2 =$　h. $9^2 - 4^2 =$　i. $17 + 6^2 =$

4. Write the next four square numbers.

64, 81, 100, _____, _____, _____, _____

5. Find the difference between these consecutive square numbers.

a. 4^2 and $5^2 =$ _____　b. 5^2 and $6^2 =$ _____

c. 6^2 and $7^2 =$ _____　d. 7^2 and $8^2 =$ _____

6. Write the missing number in this pattern.

3 + 5 + 7 + 9 + 11 + _____ + _____ + _____

7. Find the missing square numbers.

10 a. $\boxed{}^2 + 7 = \boxed{}^2$　b. $\boxed{}^2 + 9 = \boxed{}^2$

Division

1. Complete these divisions, with remainders

a. $3\overline{)172}$ r　b. $2\overline{)303}$ r　c. $5\overline{)176}$

d. $6\overline{)385}$ r　e. $4\overline{)273}$ r　f. $7\overline{)527}$

g. $4\overline{)617}$ r　h. $2\overline{)535}$ r　i. $3\overline{)440}$

2. Write the algorithm for each number sentence and then find the answer and remainder.

a. $847 \div 5 =$ 　b. $386 \div 5 =$

c. $732 \div 6 =$ 　d. $856 \div 4 =$

3. Complete each algorithm, NB. Zeros.

a. $3\overline{)4023}$ r　b. $4\overline{)2305}$ r　c. $6\overline{)5047}$ r

d. $5\overline{)6709}$ r　e. $7\overline{)1072}$ r　f. $2\overline{)3301}$ r

4. PROBLEMS

a. If I earn $240 in 8 hours, how much do I earn per hour?

☐ per hour

b. Jon rides 280 km/week. If he rides every day how many kilometres does he do each day?

☐ per hour

Capacity

Find the volume of each set of blocks.

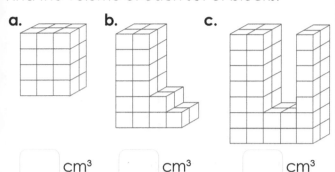

a. ☐ cm³   b. ☐ cm³   c. ☐ cm³

Write the measurement of water showing in each cylinder.

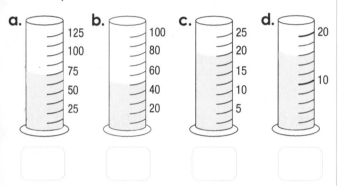

a. ☐   b. ☐   c. ☐   d. ☐

Use the displacement of water to find the mass of the apple and rock.

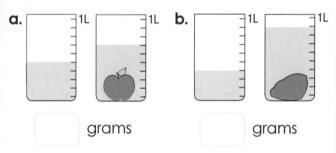

a. ☐ grams   b. ☐ grams

Write the approximate unit of capacity in L or mL for each object.

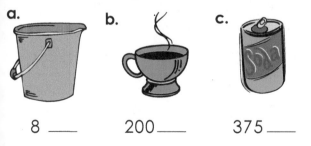

a. 8 ____   b. 200 ____   c. 375 ____

Write an equivalent mass, volume or capacity for the following.
1 cm³ = 1 gram = 1 mL

a. 600 mL= _____ g   b. 350 mL= _____cm³

c. $\frac{3}{4}$ L = _____ g   d. $\frac{1}{2}$ kg = _____cm³

e. 250mL = _____ g   f. 1 200 mL = _____ kg

Location

1. Give the co-ordinates for each shape on the grid.

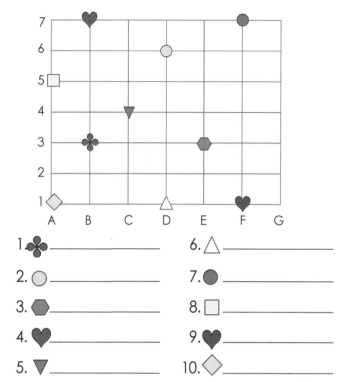

1. ♣ _____   6. △ _____

2. ○ _____   7. ● _____

3. ⬡ _____   8. ☐ _____

4. ♥ _____   9. ♥ _____

5. ▼ _____   10. ◇ _____

2. Complete the directional rose. Add the bearings too. Use the bearing bank.

360°N 0°

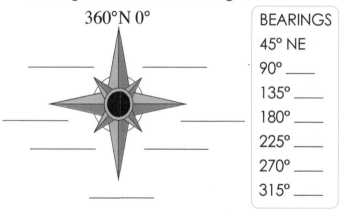

BEARINGS
45° NE
90° ____
135° ____
180° ____
225° ____
270° ____
315° ____

3. Show the path through the maze by drawing a coloured line. Write the direction or bearing for each change.

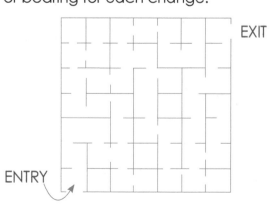

EXIT

ENTRY

_____

_____

_____ **11**

Triangular Numbers

1. Write the triangular numbers as shown by each group of circles.

a. ☐   b. ☐   c. ☐   d. ☐

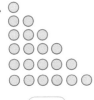 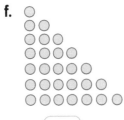

e. ☐   f. ☐

2. Write the triangular numbers for each addition. One is done for you.

1 + 2 + 3 + 4 + 5 = 15
15 is a triangular number.

a. 1 + 2 + 3 + 4 + 5 + 6 + 7 = ☐

b. 1 + 2 + 3 + 4 + 5 + 6 + 7 + 8 + 9 + 10 = ☐

c. 1 + 2 + 3 + 4 + 5 + 6 + 7 + 8 = ☐

d. 1 + 2 + 3 + 4 + 5 + 6 = ☐

3. How many counting numbers form each triangular number?

a. 66 = ☐   b. 45 = ☐   c. 91 = ☐

d. 21 = ☐   e. 120 = ☐   f. 28 = ☐

4. When you add consecutive triangular numbers the result if a square number. Add these to find square numbers. One is done for you.

△3 + △4 = 16   a. △3 + △4 = ☐

b. △7 + △8 = ☐   c. △6 + △7 = ☐

d. △9 + △10 = ☐   e. △8 + △9 = ☐

5. Write the triangular numbers **less** than 50.

Equivalent Fractions

1. Write each fraction as a percentage.

a. $\frac{12}{100}$ = _____   b. $\frac{37}{100}$ = _____   c. $\frac{52}{100}$ = _

d. $\frac{30}{100}$ = _____   e. $\frac{4}{100}$ = _____   f. $\frac{27}{100}$ = _

2. Colour each decimal fraction on the grid

a. 0.7    b. 0.2

c. 0.6   d. 0.8

e. 0.3    f. 0.5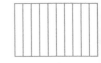

3. Write the equivalent fraction below each decimal.

a. 0.1   b. 0.7   c. 0.5   d. 0.2   e. 0.6

☐   ☐   ☐   ☐   ☐

f. 0.9   g. 0.3   h. 0.25   i. 0.75   j. 0.8

☐   ☐   ☐   ☐   ☐

4. Circle the number that is **NOT** an equivalent fraction.

a. $\frac{1}{2}$, 50%, 0.2   b. $\frac{1}{2}$, 50%, 0.4

c. $\frac{7}{10}$, 75%, $\frac{3}{4}$ d. $\frac{2}{5}$, 20%, 0.4

e. $\frac{1}{3}$, $\frac{3}{5}$, 60%   f. 80%, 0.4, $\frac{4}{5}$

5. Add the missing fractions.

a.

0.3		0.7

b.

0.7		0.8

Prisms and Pyramids

Name each 3D prism or pyramid.

a.
_____

b.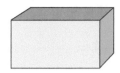
_____

c.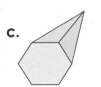
_____

d.
_____

e.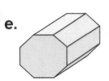
_____

f.
_____

Count the corners and faces on each 3D object.

a.

☐ faces   ☐ corners

b.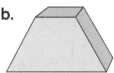

☐ faces   ☐ corners

c.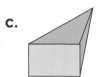

☐ faces   ☐ corners

d.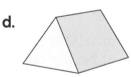

☐ faces   ☐ corners

Name the 3D object each net will make.

a.
_____

b.
_____

c.
_____

d.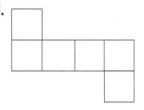
_____

Temperature

Here is a timetable showing train times from Newcastle to Gosford.

Newcastle	10:29	11:19	11:29	12:19	12:29	13:19
Civic	10:31	11:21	11:31	12:21	12:31	13:21
Wickham	10:33	11:23	11:33	12:23	12:33	13:23
Hamilton	10:36	11:26	11:36	12:26	12:36	13:26
Broadmeadow	10:39	11:29	11:39	12:29	12:39	13:29
Adamstown	10:42	---	11:42	---	12:42	---
Kotara	10:44	---	11:44	---	12:44	---
Cardiff	10:49	11:36	11:49	12:36	12:49	13:36
Cockle Creek	10:53	---	11:53	---	12:53	---
Teralba	10:56	---	11:56	---	12:56	---
Booragul	10:58	---	11:58	---	12:58	---
Fassifern	11:02	11:47	12:02	12:47	13:02	13:47
Awaba	11:07	---	12:07	---	13:07	---
Dora Creek	11:16	---	12:16	---	13:16	---
Morisset	11:20	12:03	12:20	12:47	13:02	13:47
Wyee	11:26	---	12:26	---	13:26	---
Warnervale	11:33	---	12:33	---	13:33	---
Wyong	11:39	12:19	12:39	13:19	13:39	14:19
Tuggerah	11:42	12:22	12:42	13:22	13:42	14:22
Ourimbah	11:47	---	12:47	---	13:47	---
Lisarow	11:50	---	12:50	---	13:50	---
Niagara Park	11:53	---	12:53	---	13:53	---
Narara	11:55	---	12:55	---	13:55	---
Gosford	12:00	12:36	13:00	13:36	14:00	14:36

1. How often do the trains depart Newcastle for Gosford? _____

2. If I catch the 10:49 train from Cardiff how long will it take me to get to Gosford? _____

3. How long does it take for a train from Newcastle, stopping at all stations, to reach Gosford? _____

4. What time train from Newcastle will arrive at Fassifern by thirteen minutes to two? _____

5. At what time does the last express train arrive at Wyong? _____

6. What is the difference in time between an express and an all-stations train from Newcastle to Gosford? _____

7. At what time does the first express train arrive at Morisset? _____

8. If the train goes from Gosford to Sydney the trip takes an extra 1 hour 5 minutes. What time will you arrive in Sydney if you catch the 13:19 express from Newcastle? _____

9. If the 10:29 train from Newcastle runs 35 minutes late, what time will it arrive in Gosford? _____

13

Integers

1. Write the integers for the range shown on each number line.

a. number line: -6 ... 0 +1

b. number line: -2 0 +3

c. number line: -12 ... -5

d. number line: -50 ... 0 20

2. Complete the addition and subtraction of these integers.

a. -6+7 =

b. +5-9 =

c. -7+3 =

d. -8+3 =

e. +7-12 =

f. +8-11 =

g. +7-3 =

h. -8+2 =

3. Write the temperature showing on each thermometer.

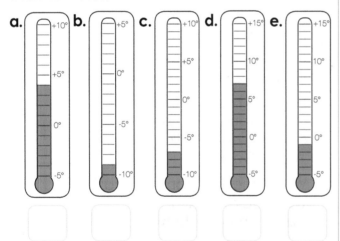

a. | b. | c. | d. | e.

4. Colour the value of the integer on each line.

a. -7   (line -5 to +5)

b. -30   (line -50 to +50)

c. +9   (line -5 to +5)

d. -250   (line -500 to +500)

e. -25   (line -50 to +50)

5. Write the number 12 **less** than these.

a. 7 =

b. -3 =

c. 6 =

Fractions

1. Write the equivalent fraction for each of these.

a. $\frac{4}{10} =$

b. $\frac{6}{8} =$

c. $\frac{30}{50} =$

d. $\frac{4}{8} =$

e. $\frac{5}{10} =$

f. $\frac{3}{12} =$

g. $\frac{2}{6} =$

h. $\frac{2}{8} =$

i. $\frac{6}{10} =$

2. To add fractions, both denominators must be the same. Change the denominators add each fraction.

a. $\frac{1}{2} + \frac{1}{4} =$

b. $\frac{2}{5} + \frac{1}{10} =$

c. $\frac{5}{8} + \frac{1}{4} =$

$\Box + \frac{1}{4} = \Box$

$\Box + \frac{1}{10} = \Box$

$\frac{5}{8} + \Box =$

d. $\frac{2}{3} + \frac{1}{6} =$

e. $\frac{3}{4} + \frac{1}{8} =$

f. $\frac{3}{10} + \frac{2}{5} =$

$\Box + \frac{1}{6} = \Box$

$\Box + \frac{1}{8} = \Box$

$\frac{3}{10} + \Box =$

3. When subtracting fractions the denomina must be the same.

a. $\frac{7}{8} - \frac{1}{4} =$

b. $\frac{7}{10} - \frac{2}{5} =$

c. $\frac{1}{2} - \frac{1}{4} =$

$\frac{7}{8} - \Box = \Box$

$\frac{7}{10} - \Box = \Box$

$\Box - \frac{1}{4} =$

d. $\frac{5}{8} - \frac{1}{2} =$

e. $\frac{3}{4} - \frac{1}{2} =$

f. $\frac{9}{10} - \frac{1}{2} =$

$\frac{5}{8} - \Box = \Box$

$\frac{3}{4} - \Box = \Box$

$\frac{9}{10} - \Box =$

4. a. $\frac{1}{2}$ of 20 =

b. $\frac{1}{4}$ of 16 =

c. $\frac{1}{5}$ of 10 =

Area

Using the relationship of length and breadth (width), find the area of each shape. (Shapes not to scale). Add cm² as the unit of measure.

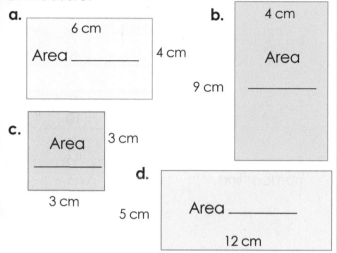

a.
6 cm
Area _____
4 cm

b.
4 cm
Area _____
9 cm

c.
Area _____
3 cm
3 cm

d.
5 cm
Area _____
12 cm

Find the length or width (not to scale).

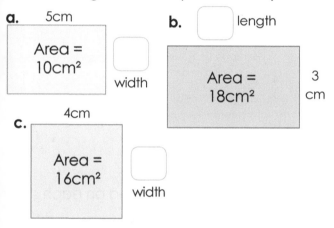

a.
5cm
Area = 10cm²
width

b.
length
Area = 18cm²
3 cm

c.
4cm
Area = 16cm²
width

Find the area of each shape. Add the areas of each rectangle.

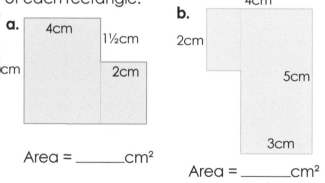

a.
4cm
1½cm
cm
2cm

Area = _____cm²

b.
4cm
2cm
5cm
3cm

Area = _____cm²

PROBLEMS

a. A rectangle has a length of 6cm and a width of 4cm. What is the area?   Area = _____cm²

b. The area of a rectangle is 24cm². If one side is 8cm what is the length of the other side?   _____cm

c. In an irregular shape, one area is 16cm². If the total area is 28cm², what is the area of the smaller shape? _____cm²

Chance

1. Analyse the chances of landing on given colours. Express each chance as a percentage.

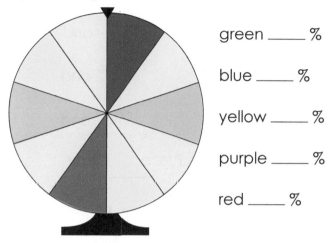

green _____ %

blue _____ %

yellow _____ %

purple _____ %

red _____ %

2. Write each chance as a fraction.

a. Tossing a head with a coin.

b. Rolling a 3 with a die.

c. Landing on a 5 on a five sectioned board.

d. Rolling a 2 or 3 with a die.

3. Roll a die 20 times and record the results.

a. What number turned up the **most**?

b. What is the percentage for that number?   _____ %
(Multiply the number, by number of times, by 5 to find %)

c. Which number has the **lowest** percentage?

d. When tossed, what numbers added to ten?

_____

5. Circle true **T** or false **F** for each chance statement.

a. 50% chance of rolling a 5.   **T** or **F**

b. To roll a 3 on a die is one chance in 6.   **T** or **F**

c. The chance of rolling an odd number with a die is 50%   **T** or **F**

d. The chance of landing a head with two coins is 25%   **T** or **F**

15

Factors

1. Write the factors for each number.

   a. 16 ☐ ☐ ☐ ☐ and ☐

   b. 20 ☐ ☐ ☐ ☐ and ☐

   c. 12 ☐ ☐ ☐ ☐ and ☐

   d. 18 ☐ ☐ ☐ ☐ and ☐

2. Circle true **T** or false **F** for each factor statement.

   a. 7 is a factor of 84.   **T** or **F**

   b. 6 is a factor of 72.   **T** or **F**

   c. 8 is a factor of 48.   **T** or **F**

   d. 9 is a factor of 89.   **T** or **F**

3. Write the number that has these factors.

   a. 1, 2, 3, 4, 6, 9, 12, 18 _____

   b. 1, 2, 3, 4, 6, 12, _____

   c. 1, 2, 3, 4, 6, 8, 12, 16, 24 _____

   d. 1, 2, 3, 5, 6, 10, 15, _____

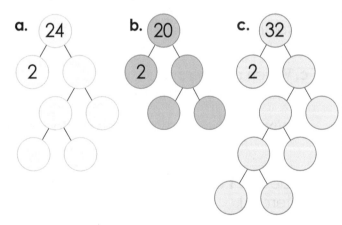

4. Complete each prime factor tree.

   a. 24   **b.** 20   **c.** 32

5. Complete the factors for each number.

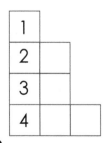
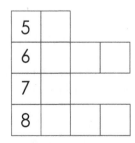

Decimals and Fractions

1. Add the missing fractions.

   a.

| 0.2 | | 0.4 | | | 0.7 | 0.8 | | 1 |

   b.
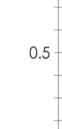

| $\frac{1}{8}$ | $\frac{1}{4}$ | | $\frac{1}{2}$ | | $\frac{7}{8}$ | 1 |

   c.

| $\frac{3}{10}$ | $\frac{2}{5}$ | $\frac{1}{2}$ | | | $\frac{9}{10}$ | 1 |

2. Match each fraction to its position on the number line.

$\frac{2}{5}$ 0   0.7

$\frac{1}{4}$ $\frac{1}{2}$

0.3   0.5 $\frac{3}{5}$

$\frac{4}{5}$ $\frac{1}{5}$

0.9   1 $\frac{3}{4}$

3. Write the fraction coloured on each shape.

   a.   **b.**   **c.**   **d.**

   ☐   ☐   ☐   ☐

4. Add these decimal number sentences.

   a. 0.37 + 1.24 + 1.08 + 1.12 = ☐

   b. 0.14 + 0.33 + 1.45 + 0.2 = ☐

   c. 1.15 + 0.16 + 1.15 + 2.77 = ☐

   d. 0.35 + 0.45 + 1.03 + 1.45 = ☐

5. Circle the **larger** fraction.

   a. $\frac{3}{10}$ or $\frac{3}{5}$ **b.** 25% or $\frac{1}{3}$ **c.** $\frac{5}{8}$ or

   d. $\frac{6}{100}$ or 3%   **e.** $\frac{3}{8}$ or $\frac{3}{4}$ **f.** $\frac{1}{2}$ or

Angles

Name each angle.

a.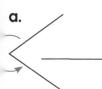
_____

b.
_____

c.
_____

d.
_____

e.
_____

f.
_____

Which angle is showing on each protractor?

a.
_____

b.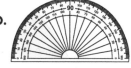
_____

c.
_____

d.
_____

Use a protractor to measure each angle.

a.

b.

c.

The three angles of a triangle add to 180°. Find the size of the third angle.

a.
80°
45°   ?

b.
?
30°

c.
110°   ?
30°

A straight line is 180°. Find the **complimentary** angle size.

a.
72°

b.
110°

c.
60°

Data

Read the data on the graph and then complete the activities.

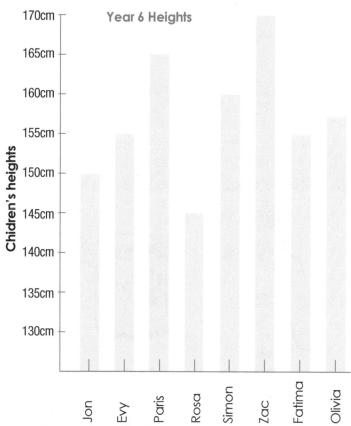

1. Who is the **tallest** in the group? _____

2. Who is the **shortest** in the group? _____

3. How much **taller** is Paris than Evy? _____

4. What is the range of heights? _____

5. Who is the **shortest** boy? _____

6. How much **taller** is Zac than Jon? _____

7. If Evy's dad is 30cm **taller** than her, how tall is he?   _____

8. Zac's mum is 15cm **shorter** than he is. How tall is his mum?   _____

9. Zac has a twin sister who is 12cm **shorter** than he is. How tall is she?   _____

10. Paris is 25cm **taller** than her younger sister. How tall is her sister? _____

11. What is the **average** height of the girls?

12. What is the **average** height of all the children?

17

Money

1. Write each fraction or decimal as a percentage.

a. $\dfrac{72}{100}$ = ____ %   **b.** $\dfrac{18}{100}$ = ____ %   **c.** $\dfrac{48}{100}$ = ____ %

d. $\dfrac{1}{2}$ = ____ %   **e.** $\dfrac{3}{4}$ = ____ %   **f.** $\dfrac{2}{5}$ = ____ %

g. 0.7 = ____ %   **h.** 0.6 = ____ %   **i.** 0.25 = ____ %

2. Write the discount price for each item.

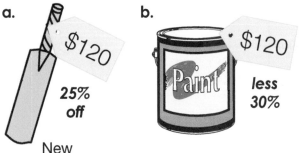

a. $120   25% off
New Price $_____

b. $120 less 30%
New Price $_____

c. $850   20% off
New Price $_____

d. $1200   50% off
New Price $_____

3. Find the percentages for each sum of money.

a. 10% of $50 = _____   **b.** 25% of $80 = _____

c. 50% of $1000 = _____   **d.** 10% of $200 = _____

e. 25% of $200 = _____   **f.** 50% of $40 = _____

4. a. $800 was the price of Lucy's new mobile phone. If it was reduced by 20%, how much did she pay for the phone?

Price = $ _____

b. Harry was offered a 25% discount on his holiday if he paid that day. The original cost was $1 000. How much did it cost Harry to pay that day?

Price = $ _____

Number Patterns

This graph can be used to show multiples numbers.

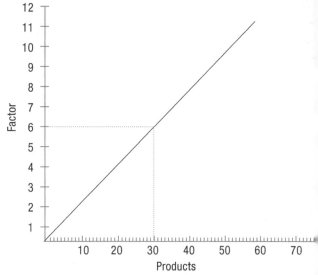

Factor / Products

1. Show these multiples on the graph. 5 x 6 = 30 is already done.

a. 4 x 6 = ☐   **b.** 6 x 6 = ☐

c. 8 x 6 = ☐   **d.** 3 x 6 = ☐

e. 7 x 6 = ☐   **f.** 10 x 6 = ☐

g. 11 x 6 = ☐   **h.** 9 x 6 = ☐

2. Extend each pattern.

Rule	Pattern
+52	18, 70, ___, ___, ___
x3	3, 6, 9, ___, ___, ___
-16	178, 162, ___, ___, ___
÷2	64, 32, ___, ___, ___

3. Extend the decimal patterns.

a. 0.6, 1.2, 1.8, _____, _____, _____, _____

b. 0.15, 0.2, 0.25, _____, _____, _____, _____

c. 4.66, 3.96, 3.26, _____, _____, _____, _____

4. Fill in the missing **square** numbers.

4, _____, _____, _____, _____, _____, 64

5. Fill in the missing **triangular** numbers.

3, _____, _____, _____, _____, _____, 36

Rotational Symmetry

te the number of times each shape matches
t rotates through 360°.

1.

2.

3.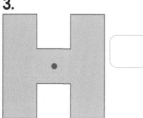

4.

5.

6.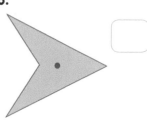

7.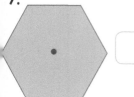

8.

9.

10.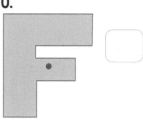

11.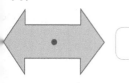

12.

Draw the other half of each shape and then
add the centre point.

a.

b.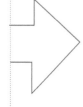

24 Hour Time

1. Add the compass points and bearings
to the rose.

N 360°

2. Using the compass complete the following.

   a. If north has a bearing of 0°,
   what is the bearing of **east**? _____

   b. What is the bearing for **south**? _____

   c. How many degrees
   between north and south? _____

   d. In what direction will you travel
   if you move 45° past south? _____

   e. Which point has a bearing
   of 270°? _____

   f. How many degrees between
   south and south-west? _____

   g. What direction will 90° **more**
   more than south-east be? _____

3. If you are in a boat and change from
north-west to north, through how
many degrees will you pass? _____

4. Use the co-ordinates to draw each shape
on the grid.

D4 🌼

B3 ✪

C5 ◉

A1 ◆

E4 ❖

F2 ⬤

G3 ❆

19

Order of Operations

1. Complete each operation. Do brackets first.

a. 4 x (3+2) = _____   **b.** (2+4) x 3 = _____

c. (5-2) x 6 = _____   **d.** 5 x (4+3) = _____

e. 7 x (8-4) = _____   **f.** (6x2) ÷ 4 = _____

g. (7x6) ÷ 2 = _____   **h.** 25 ÷ (8-3) = _____

2. Do brackets first and then work from left to right.

a. 27 ÷ 3 x (4+2) = _____   **b.** (32÷8) x 5 = _____

c. 8 x 2 - (6x2) = _____   **d.** 13 x 3 - (5x7) = _____

e. 24 ÷ 3 + (6x3) = _____   **f.** 8 + (4x3) ÷ 2 = _____

g. 4 + (8x3) ÷ 4 = _____   **h.** 14 + (2+6) x 3 = _____

3. Write true (**T**) or false (**F**) for each of comparison.   **T/F**

a. (32-7) ÷ 5 + 9 - 3 = (6x3) + (12÷2) - 13 _____

b. (6x4) ÷ 8 x 7 + 3 = (7x2) + 4 - (9÷3) _____

c. 21 ÷ 3 + (16-8) x 2 = 3 x 3 + (9-3) + 8 _____

d. 15 ÷ 5 + (24÷3) - 5 = (7x2) + 4 - (36÷3) _____

e. 9 x (3+7) ÷ 5 + 2 = (27-9) ÷ 3 + (2x6) _____

4. Remember 'of' means multiply.

a. $\frac{1}{4}$ of 32 = ☐   **b.** $\frac{1}{2}$ of 36 = ☐

c. $\frac{1}{3}$ of 39 = ☐   **d.** $\frac{2}{5}$ of 30 = ☐

e. $\frac{7}{10}$ of 70 = ☐   **f.** $\frac{3}{8}$ of 40 = ☐

5. Brackets first then 'of', division, addition and subtraction last.

a. (2x4) + $\frac{1}{2}$ of 14 + (15÷5) = _____

b. $\frac{1}{2}$ of 20 + $\frac{1}{3}$ of 21 - (6x2) = _____

c. (42÷6) x 2 + $\frac{1}{4}$ of 20 - 7 = _____

20

Fractions

1. Write the fraction for the coloured part in each shape

a.   **b.**   **c.** 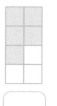   **d.**

☐   ☐   ☐   ☐

2. Write equivalent fractions.

a. $\frac{2}{5} = \frac{☐}{10}$ **b.** $\frac{1}{4} = \frac{☐}{8}$ **c.** $\frac{2}{6} = \frac{☐}{}$

d. $\frac{8}{10} = \frac{☐}{5}$ **e.** $\frac{3}{4} = \frac{☐}{8}$ **f.** $\frac{3}{5} = \frac{☐}{}$

g. $\frac{8}{10} = \frac{☐}{5}$ **h.** $\frac{1}{2} = \frac{☐}{10}$ **i.** $\frac{1}{2} = \frac{☐}{}$

3. Add the fractions. Change one denominator to an equivalent fraction.

a. $\frac{2}{3} + \frac{1}{6} =$ **b.** $\frac{1}{8} + \frac{1}{4} =$ **c.** $\frac{1}{2} + \frac{3}{10} =$

☐ + $\frac{1}{6}$ = ☐ $\frac{1}{8}$ + ☐ = ☐   ☐ + $\frac{3}{10}$ =

d. $\frac{1}{5} + \frac{3}{10} =$ **e.** $\frac{3}{4} + \frac{1}{8} =$ **f.** $\frac{3}{10} + \frac{3}{5} =$

☐ + $\frac{3}{10}$ = ☐   ☐ + $\frac{1}{8}$ = ☐ $\frac{3}{10}$ + ☐ =

4. Complete each subtraction. Change one denominator.

a. $\frac{5}{8} - \frac{1}{4} =$ **b.** $\frac{7}{10} - \frac{1}{5} =$ **c.** $\frac{1}{2} - \frac{3}{10} =$

$\frac{5}{8}$ - ☐ = ☐ $\frac{7}{10}$ - ☐ = ☐   ☐ - $\frac{3}{10}$ =

d. $\frac{7}{8} - \frac{3}{4} =$ **e.** $\frac{9}{10} - \frac{2}{5} =$ **f.** $\frac{2}{3} - \frac{1}{6} =$

$\frac{7}{8}$ - ☐ = ☐ $\frac{9}{10}$ - ☐ =   ☐ - $\frac{1}{6}$ =

Triangles

Draw a line from each triangle to its name.

a.

b.

scalene

equilateral

c.

right angle

d.

isosceles

Measure the sides of each triangle. Write the perimeter and the name of each triangle.

a.

perimeter

_____

_____

b.

perimeter

_____

_____

c.

perimeter

_____

_____

d.

perimeter

_____

_____

Remember, three angles of a triangle add to 180°. Find the size of the third angle in each triangle.

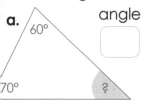

a.

60°

angle ☐

70°

?

b.

?

80°

angle ☐

30°

c.

?

angle ☐

30°

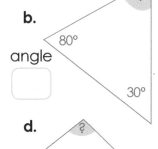

d.

?

55°   45°

angle ☐

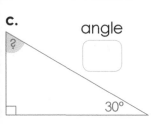

a. All angles in an equilateral triangle equal   _____

b. An isosceles triangle has _____ equal angles and sides.

c. A _____ triangle has one angle of 90°.

Graphs

1. Make a picture graph to show this data.

Sold Cartons of Apple Juice.

Mon	Tues	Wed	Thurs	Fri	Sat	Sun
105	95	120	125	100	110	115

Picture Graph ■ = cartons	
Mon	
Tues	
Wed	
Thurs	
Fri	
Sat	
Sun	

2. What does a picture graph tell us?

_____

3. Name three other types of graphs you could use to show this data.

_____

_____

_____

4. Here is a bar graph showing the mode of transport to work for 80 people.

Walk	Car	Bus	Train

a. How many travel by train? _____

b. How many use their car? _____

c. How many **more** people walk than travel by bus? _____

d. How many people go to work on public transport? _____

21

Decimal Fractions

1. Write the decimal fraction that falls half-way between each number.

a. 0.6 _____ 0.8   **b.** 0.25 _____ 0.75

c. 0.68 _____ 0.72   **d.** 0.85 _____ 0.89

e. 1.75 _____ 2.25   **f.** 1.336 _____ 1.434

g. 0.883 _____ 1.283   **h.** 1.825 _____ 1.975

2. Match each fraction to its place on the number line.

a. 0.65   0
c. 1.05
e. 0.75   0.5
g. 1.25
i. 0.15   1
k. 0.35   1.5

b. 0.25
d. 1.3
f. 0.45
h. 0.55
j. 1.45
l. 1.10

3. Write the decimal fraction for each of these.

a. $\frac{2}{10}$ = _____   **b.** $\frac{7}{10}$ = _____   **c.** $\frac{2}{5}$ = _____

d. $\frac{3}{4}$ = _____   **e.** $\frac{5}{8}$ = _____   **f.** $1\frac{1}{2}$ = _____

g. $\frac{3}{5}$ = _____   **h.** $\frac{9}{10}$ = _____   **i.** $\frac{1}{4}$ = _____

4. Write the place value of each circled number – ones, tenths, hundredths or thousandths.

a. 0 . 7②1   **b.** 2 .③6 5   **c.** 1 . 7 5②

_____   _____   _____

d. ③. 6 6 5   **e.** 3 . 1 5②   **f.** 7 . 6⑤3

_____   _____   _____

Decimals

Keep the decimal point in line, under each other, when writing decimals.

always align

```
   2.7
   1.3
 +1.5
_____
     .
```

1. Add these decimal fractions.

a. 32.54   **b.** 11.39   **c.** 81.7
 +63.17   +2.86   +12.9

d. 38.215   **e.** 14.134   **f.** 27.6
 +1.753   +38.583   +14.88

g. 62.384   **h.** 42.734   **i.** 24.68
   11.170   19.168   12.79
 +62.493   +7.059   +0.82

2. Find the difference between each decimal fraction.

a. 83.75   **b.** 49.336   **c.** 33.5
 -12.83   -12.798   -12.7

d. 447.38   **e.** 37.675   **f.** 227.6
 -128.84   -19.057   -129.3

3. Add or subtract each sum of money. Watch the signs.

a. $275.63   **b.** $63.77   **c.** $673.
 +$185.77   +$48.88   +$295.
 $. $. $.

d. $726.66   **e.** $529.63   **f.** $983.
 -$133.72   -$444.84   -$618.
 $. $. $.

Length

Write the approximate unit of length (mm, cm, m or ha) for each object.

a.

12 _____

b.

15 _____

c.

38 _____

d.

15 _____

e.
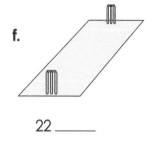
25 _____

f.
22 _____

Arrange each group of lengths in order, **shortest** to **longest**.

a. 47mm, 4cm, 43m, 46mm, 4km, 42m

_____

b. 0.72km, 7.87m, 730cm, 989mm, 780m, 0.7km

_____

c. 52mm, 5cm, 0.51m, 0.005km, 51.5mm

_____

Find the length of each line. Line scale used, 1 cm = 8 km.

a. _____ ☐ km

b. _____ ☐ km

c. _____ ☐ km

Write the equivalent lengths or distances.

a. 30mm = _____ cm

b. 4km = _____ m

c. 500m = _____ km

d. ☐ cm = $\frac{1}{4}$ m

e. ☐ cm = 6m

f. ☐ m = 2km

Distance and Time

1. Use the before and after readings on each odometer to calculate the distance travelled.

a.
BEFORE

AFTER

TRIP
☐☐☐

b.
BEFORE

AFTER

TRIP
☐☐☐

2. Write the speed showing on each odometer.

a.

☐

b.

☐

c.

☐

d.

☐

3. Mark the speed a car needs to travel to cover the allotted time.

a. 100 km in 1 hour
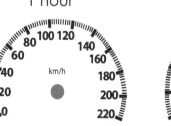

b. 120 km in 2 hours

c. 180 km in 2 hours

d. 150 km in 3 hours

Place Value

Two-digit Multiplication

1. Round off each number to the **nearest million**.

a. 18 725 816

b. 72 183 625

_____ _____

c. 88 598 312

d. 43 678 298

_____ _____

2. Identify the place value of each circled numeral.

a. 3 7④1 625

b. 7 ②64 183

_____ _____

c. 24 68⑨ 758

d. 87 ②16 385

_____ _____

3. Write the number showing on each abacus.

a.    b.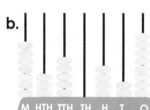

M HTH TTH TH H T O   M HTH TTH TH H T O

_____ _____

4. Write the numeral for the expanded number.

a. 2 000 000 + 400 000 + 20 000
+ 8 000 + 700 + 90 + 7 = _____

b. 6 000 000 + 800 000 + 90 000
+ 6 000 + 200 + 40 + 6 = _____

c. 40 000 000 + 2 000 000 + 700 000
+ 50 000 + 8 000 + 900 + 60 + 4 = _____

5. Write the written number in numerals.

a. Twenty-two million, seven hundred and eighty-seven thousand, four hundred and forty-four.

_____

b. Thirty nine million, three hundred and seventy-two thousand, eight hundred and ninety-four.

24 _____

1. Find the product.

a.   3 2 6
   x 2 0
   _____

b.   4 1 7
   x 1 0
   _____

c.   6
   x
   ____

d.   4 1 5
   x 5 0
   _____

e.   6 1 6
   x 7 0
   _____

f.   3
   x
   ____

2. When finding these products, add two zeros before multiplying.

a.   3 2 6
   x 2 0 0
   _____

b.   3 3 5
   x 2 0 0
   _____

c.   4
   x 3 0
   ____

d.   3 1 6
   x 4 0 0
   _____

e.   8 6 1
   x 1 0 0
   _____

f.   3
   x 5 0
   ____

3. Multiply the thousands by the multiples of ten and one hundered. Remember: Add zeros for correct place values.

a. 3 0 0 0
   x 6 0
   _____

b. 4 0 0 0
   x 2 0 0
   _____

c. 7 0 0
   x 3 0

d. 5 0 0 0
   x 7 0
   _____

e. 2 0 0 0
   x 7 0 0
   _____

f. 6 0 0
   x 5 0

4. a. A Highway Patrol Officer booked 50 speeding motorists. If the fines were $275 each, how much was paid in fines?

_____

b. 30 coal trains each pulled 1 235 tonnes. How much coal did the 30 trains pull?

_____

Mass

Use the Mass Bank to write an approximate mass for each object.

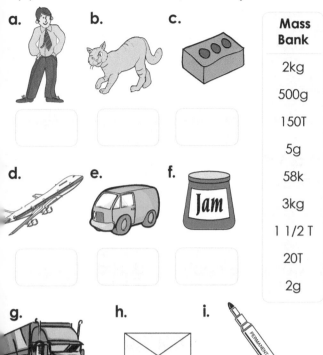

a.

b.

c.

Mass Bank
2kg
500g
150T
5g
58k
3kg
1 1/2 T
20T
2g

d.

e.

f. Jam

g.

h.

i.

Write each mass in kilograms.

a. 3 850g **b.** 7 000g **c.** 900g **d.** 7 183g

_____ _____ _____ _____

e. 4 500g **f.** 7 750g **g.** 430g **h.** 8 361g

_____ _____ _____ _____

A jar has a mass of 380 grams, which includes contents. The mass of the jar is 150 grams.

What is the mass of the contents? _____

A can of peaches has a gross mass of 895 grams. The net mass is 750 grams.

What is the mass of the can? _____

Write each tonnage in kilograms.

a. 4.7 tonnes _____   **b.** 7.2 tonnes _____

c. 4.35 tonnes _____   **d.** 0.92 tonnes _____

e. 0.83 tonnes _____   **f.** 1.04 tonnes _____

Timetables

Here is a timetable showing train times from Bankstown to the city.

Bankstown	11:30	11:45	12:00	12:15	12:30	12:45
Punchbowl	11:33	11:48	12:03	12:18	12:33	12:48
Wiley Park	11:35	11:50	12:05	12:20	12:35	12:50
Lakemba	11:37	11:52	12:07	12:22	12:37	12:52
Belmore	11:39	11:54	12:09	12:24	12:39	12:54
Campsie	11:41	11:56	12:11	12:26	12:41	12:56
Canterbury	11:44	11:59	12:14	12:29	12:44	12:59
Hurlstone Park	11:46	12:01	12:16	12:31	12:46	13:01
Dulwich Hill	11:48	12:03	12:18	12:33	12:48	13:03
Marrickville	11:51	12:06	12:21	12:36	12:51	13:06
Sydenham	11:55	12:10	12:25	12:40	12:55	13:10
St Peters	11:57	12:12	12:27	12:42	12:57	13:12
Erskineville	11:59	12:14	12:29	12:44	12:59	13:14
Redfern	12:02	12:17	12:32	12:47	13:02	13:17
Central	12:06	12:21	12:36	12:51	13:06	13:21
Town Hall	12:09	12:24	12:39	12:54	13:09	13:24
Wynyard	12:12	12:27	12:42	12:57	13:12	13:27
Circular Quay	12:15	12:30	12:45	13:00	13:15	13:30
St James	12:18	12:33	12:48	13:03	13:18	13:33
Museum	12:20	12:35	12:50	13:05	13:20	13:35

1. How often do trains run from Bankstown to the city? _____

2. If you catch the 12:05 train from Wiley Park, what time will you arrive at Circular Quay? _____

3. What time train from Bankstown will arrive in Sydenham by five to one? _____

4. How long is that trip? _____

5. If the 12 o'clock train from Bankstown is 5 minutes early, what time will it arrive at Erskineville? _____

6. To catch a train from Central to Newcastle at a quarter past one, what time train from Lakemba will you need to catch to Central? _____

7. How long is the journey from Bankstown to Museum Station? _____

8. If the 12:15 train is delayed 8 minutes, what time will it arrive at St Peters Station? _____

9. If the 12:15 train is 8 minutes late leaving Bankstown and the next train is on time, how long will you need to wait for the next train _____

10. If a train leaves Marrickville at 12:51 what time did it leave Bankstown? _____

Prime Factors

1. Draw a line from each prime number to that word.

(5) (4) (7) (6) (3)

(12)   (8)

(13)   PRIME NUMBER   (9)

(18)   (11)

(17) (23) (21) (29) (19)

2. Write the factors for each number.

a. 2 ☐   **b.** 7 ☐   **c.** 11 ☐

d. 13 ☐   **e.** 17 ☐   **f.** 5 ☐

g. 29 ☐   **h.** 19 ☐   **i.** 31 ☐

3. How many factors did each of the above numbers have? _____

What number was common to all the numbers? _____

4. Write the prime numbers **less** than 30.

_____

5. Classify each number as either **prime** or **composite**.

a. 25 _____   **b.** 37 _____

c. 81 _____   **d.** 71 _____

d. 51 _____   **e.** 39 _____

6. Complete each factor tree to find the **prime factors**.

  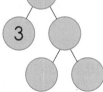

a. (30) — 2, ...   **b.** (27) — 3, ...   **c.** (18) — 3, ...

Division

1. Write as an algorithm each number sentence. Complete the division and write the remainder as a fraction.

a. 847 ÷ 3 =   **b.** 712 ÷ 5 =   **c.** 689 ÷ 6

$$\overline{\smash{)}}\,r \qquad \overline{\smash{)}}\,r \qquad \overline{\smash{)}}\,r$$

d. 6093 ÷ 6 =   **e.** 5935 ÷ 2 =   **f.** 7733 ÷ 3

$$\overline{\smash{)}}\,r \qquad \overline{\smash{)}}\,r \qquad \overline{\smash{)}}\,r$$

2. Complete each four-digit division. Write the remainder as a fraction.

a. 5)3817 r   **b.** 4)2361 r   **c.** 3)246

d. 6)6127 r   **e.** 8)3821 r   **f.** 7)626

3. PROBLEMS

a. If you earn $1 277 per week, how much will you earn in a day? I work 5 days/week.

b. Divide 12 dozen roses into 7 display. How many displays?

4. Divide each number sentence. Note the pattern.

a. 42 ÷ 6 = _____   **b.** 81 ÷ 9 = _____

420 ÷ 6 = _____   810 ÷ 9 = _____

4200 ÷ 6 = _____   8100 ÷ 9 = _____

c. 55 ÷ 11 = _____   **d.** 36 ÷ 4 = _____

550 ÷ 11 = _____   360 ÷ 4 = _____

5500 ÷ 11 = _____   3600 ÷ 4 = _____

3D Shapes

Draw the shape you would see if each 3D object was cut along the dotted line.

a.

b.

c.

d.

e.

f.

Name the 3D object that can be made by each net.

a.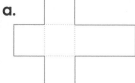

_____

b.

_____

_____

c.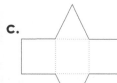

_____

_____

d.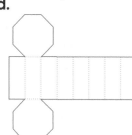

_____

_____

Location

Here is a map of Littleton. Use the landmarks and co-ordinates to find locations.

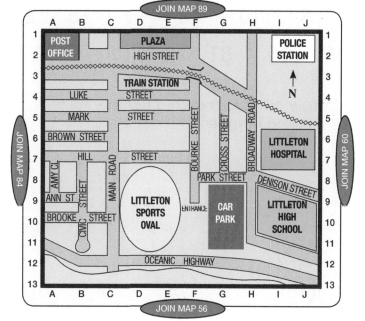

1. Give the co-ordinates for the following:

    a. Post Office _____   **b.** Police Station _____

    c. Plaza _____   **d.** Train Station _____

    e. Hospital _____   **f.** Car Park _____

2. Name the specific landmarks at these co-ordinates.

    a. D9 _____   **b.** I10 _____

    c. D3 _____   **d.** F9 _____

3. In what direction does the railway line run through the town?

    _____

4. In what direction does Denison Street run?

    _____

5. If you leave the Plaza to go to the Train Station in which direction would you walk?

    _____

6. Give the co-ordinates for the railway underpass. _____

7. Give the co-ordinates for the following intersections.

    a. Main Road and Hill Street _____

    b. Bourke and Park Streets _____

    c. Main Road and Brooke Street _____

    d. Ann and Amy Streets _____

27

Square Numbers

1. Circle only the square numbers.

$$5 \quad 10 \quad 16 \quad 9 \quad 18 \quad 25$$

$$36 \quad 84 \quad 81 \quad 64 \quad 9 \quad 100$$

2. Draw a line to match a number to its squared number.

3^2 9 5^2 81 2^2

64

7^2 100 49 4^2 25 8^2

16 4

10^2 9^2 36 6^2

3. Add composite and square numbers.

a. $4^2 + 9 =$ ◻ **b.** $9^2 + 7 =$ ◻ **c.** $3^2 + 11 =$ ◻

d. $5^2 + 6^2 =$ ◻ **e.** $7^2 + 3 =$ ◻ **f.** $8^2 + 7 =$ ◻

g. $9 + 2^2 =$ ◻ **h.** $10^2 + 7^2 =$ ◻ **i.** $21^2 + 3 =$ ◻

4. Find the difference between squared numbers and composite numbers.

a. $8^2 - 12 =$ ◻ **b.** $7^2 - 9 =$ ◻ **c.** $81 - 5^2 =$ ◻

d. $100 - 3^2 =$ ◻ **e.** $64 - 4^2 =$ ◻ **f.** $36 - 2^2 =$ ◻

g. $6^2 - 9 =$ ◻ **h.** $7^2 - 8 =$ ◻ **i.** $11^2 - 50 =$ ◻

5. Find the difference between each squared number.

a. $9^2 - 3^2 =$ ◻ **b.** $7^2 - 4^2 =$ ◻ **c.** $6^2 - 2^2 =$ ◻

d. $8^2 - 4^2 =$ ◻ **e.** $8^2 - 6^2 =$ ◻ **f.** $5^2 - 3^2 =$ ◻

g. $6^2 - 4^2 =$ ◻ **h.** $10^2 - 3^2 =$ ◻ **i.** $9^2 - 7^2 =$ ◻

---

1. Multiply each decimal fraction by 10.

a. $6.37 \times 10 =$ ◻ **b.** $24.36 \times 10 =$ ◻

c. $0.03 \times 10 =$ ◻ **d.** $0.35 \times 10 =$ ◻

e. $0.001 \times 10 =$ ◻ **f.** $1.03 \times 10 =$ ◻

2. Multiply each decimal fraction by 100.

a. $7.21 \times 100 =$ ◻ **b.** $0.637 \times 100 =$ ◻

c. $0.03 \times 100 =$ ◻ **d.** $21.04 \times 100 =$ ◻

e. $0.35 \times 100 =$ ◻ **f.** $1.003 \times 100 =$ ◻

3. Multiply each decimal by 1 000.

a. $0.03 \times 1000 =$ ◻ **b.** $12.3 \times 1000 =$ ◻

c. $0.052 \times 1000 =$ ◻ **d.** $0.75 \times 1000 =$ ◻

e. $0.007 \times 1000 =$ ◻ **f.** $0.073 \times 1000 =$ ◻

> When dividing decimals by ten, one hundred or one thousand move the decimal point to the left and add zero where needed.

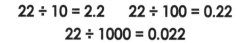

$$22 \div 10 = 2.2 \qquad 22 \div 100 = 0.22$$
$$22 \div 1000 = 0.022$$

4. Divide each decimal fraction by 10 or 1[

a. $3.7 \div 10 =$ ◻ **b.** $6.33 \div 10 =$ ◻

c. $0.3 \div 10 =$ ◻ **d.** $2.15 \div 100 =$ ◻

e. $1.7 \div 10 =$ ◻ **f.** $0.4 \div 1000 =$ ◻

4. DIVISION PROBLEMS

a. 350 girls divided into teams of 10 for the Games Carnival. How many teams will play in the carnival?

b. In a stamp albu a page holds 1C stamps. If the album has 256 pages how mar stamps will it ho

_____ teams

$$10 \overline{) 350}$$

$$10 \times 256 = \text{\_\_\_\_}$$

stam

Area

Calculate the area of each shape. Divide each shape into rectangles and apply the formula length x width (breadth) L X W = Area.

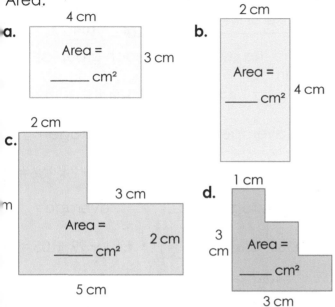

a.
4 cm
Area = _____ cm²
3 cm

b.
2 cm
Area = _____ cm²
4 cm

c.
2 cm
3 cm
Area = _____ cm²
2 cm
5 cm

d.
1 cm
3 cm
Area = _____ cm²
3 cm

To find the area of a triangle multiply height x ½ base. Find the area of each triangle. (Don't forget the unit of area = cm².)

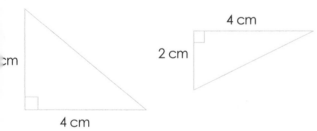

a. Area = _____

b. Area = _____
4 cm
2 cm
4 cm

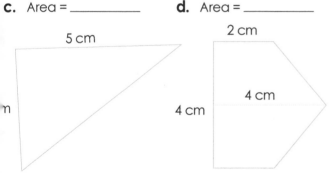

c. Area = _____
5 cm

d. Area = _____
2 cm
4 cm
4 cm

Write the square centimetres in square metres (m²).

a. 10 000cm² = _____   b. 30 000cm² = _____

c. 7 500cm² = _____   d. 5 000cm² = _____

A rectangle has one side 8 cm and the other 6 cm. What is the area? _____

A triangle has a base of 8 cm and a height of 5 cm. What is its area? _____

Chance

1. Match the chance of each event happening on the vertical probability scale.

Next baby born is a boy		Rain tomorrow
Roll 5 on a dice	NEVER 0	Night will fall
A volcano erupts	0.5	Christmas in July
Monday - school		Train is on time
Win at footy on Saturday	1 CERTAIN	Drive Dad's car

2. Write the possibility for each circumstance, as a fraction.

   a. Toss a head with a coin. ▢

   b. Roll an odd number with a die. ▢

   c. Toss two heads with three coins. ▢

   d. Roll a one with a die. ▢

3. Write the possible outcome for each as a percentage.

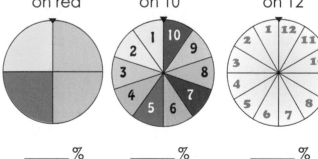

a. land on red   b. land on 10   c. land on 12

_____ %   _____ %   _____ %

4. Here is a 'feely bag' with ten discs. Write the chance of drawing the colours as a percentage.

   a. red _____ %

   b. blue _____ %

   c. green _____ %

   d. yellow _____ % **29**

Integers

1. Fill in the missing integers on each line.

a.
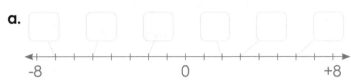

b.

c.

2. Find the difference between each set of integers.

a. -5 and + 5 = _____   **b.** -8 and + 9 = _____

c. -19 and - 9 = _____   **d.** -12 and 0 = _____

e. -25 and + 8 = _____   **f.** -32 and + 10 = _____

3. Record the temperature on each thermometer. Don't forget + or – °C.

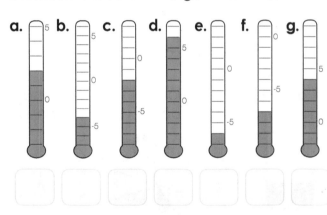

a. **b.** **c.** **d.** **e.** **f.** **g.**

4. Order each group of numbers, **smallest** to **largest**.

a. +3, -6, +7, -2, -8, +5, -5, -4

_____

b. +20, -6, +4, -8, -12, +5, +9, -14

_____

c. +0.3, -.0.5, -.0.7, -.0.2, +2, -1, 0

30 _____

Averages

Add the group of scores and then divide by the number in that group to find the average or 'mid' number of the scores.

18
24
35
27
104

104÷4
Avera
26

1. Find the average for each group of numbers.

a. 6 + 7 + 9 + 14 = ☐   **b.** 17 + 15 +7 = ☐

average= _____   average= _____

c. 22 + 93 + 84 + 9 = ☐   **d.** 82 + 74 + 36 = ☐

average= _____   average= _____

e. 35 + 36 + 37 = ☐   **f.** 81 + 99 +105 = ☐

average= _____   average= _____

2. Sometimes averages include a decimal Find each average to two decimal plac

a. 72 + 49 + 36 = ☐   **b.** 64 + 48 + 34 = ☐

average= _____   average= _____

c. 47 + 3 + 64 + 19 = ☐   average= _____

d. 0.64 + 1.2 + 3.5 = ☐   average= _____

3. Find the **average** mass of these sheep.

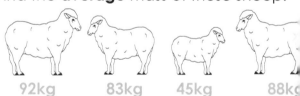

92kg   83kg   45kg   88kg

Average mass = _____ kg

4. Calculate the **average** height of the Smith family.

1.82m   1.71m   1.62m   1.48m   1.42

Average family height = _____ m

5. PROBLEM
Jon scored 42 runs Saturday, 62 Sunday, 58 last week and 40 the week before. What is his batting average for the four games?   _____

Volume and Capacity

Remember, one litre of water will balance a one kilogram mass. Write the mass of each measure of water.

a. 250mL = _____g **b.** 700mL = _____g

c. 1000mL = _____g **d.** 1500mL = _____g

e. 550mL = _____g **f.** $8\frac{1}{2}$ Litres = _____g

Write each capacity as a decimal.

a. 3750mL = _____L **b.** 2250mL = _____L

c. 1050mL = _____L **d.** 350mL = _____L

e. 9483mL = _____L **f.** 795 mL = _____L

Find the volume of each object.
(One block = 10 grams)

a. 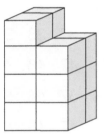   **b.**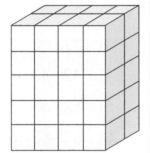

Volume =_____ g   Volume =_____ g

Write the volume or capacity for each object. (cm³, m³, or mL)

a.    **b.**    **c.**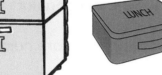

3 000_____   2 _____   400 _____

Measure the mass of the object by its displacement.

a.   **b.**

Volume   Volume
displaced =_____ mL   displaced =_____ L

Orange's   Mass of each
mass =   _____ g   marble =   _____ g

Data

The data shows tidal movements over one week.

Days	Sun	Mon	Tues	Wed	Thurs	Fri	Sat
High Tide	1.8m	2.1m	1.9m	1.7m	1.8m	2.3m	1.95m
Low Tide	0.2m	0.3m	0.4m	0.1m	0.5m	0.7m	0.0m

1. Dot plot the above data on this graph and join the dots to make a two line graph. Show high tides in blue and low tides in red.

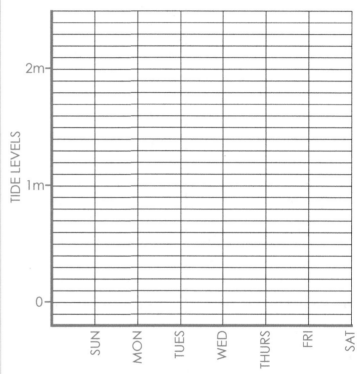

2. On which day was there a **greater** tidal difference? _____

3. Which day or days had the **lowest** tidal difference? _____

4. Which days had the **same** high tide levels? _____

5. How many high tides were over 1.8 metres?

6. Which days had a tidal range of 1.6 metres?

_____ _____ _____

7. What was the **average high** tide level for the week? _____

8. What was the week's **average** for **low** tide levels?

Composite Numbers

Composite numbers have more than two factors.

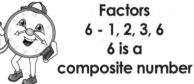

Factors
6 - 1, 2, 3, 6
6 is a
composite number

1. List the factors for these numbers.

a. 24 ⬜⬜⬜⬜ and ⬜

b. 15 ⬜⬜ and ⬜

c. 28 ⬜⬜⬜ and ⬜

d. 32 ⬜⬜⬜ and ⬜

2. Complete the factors for each number.

a. 2

b. 3

c. 9

d. 10

e. 13

f. 17

g. 8

h. 21

i. 15

3. Write the composite numbers **less** than 15.

_____

4. Write the prime numbers **less** than 20.

_____

5. Write the numbers that will divide into each of these.

a. 12 ⬜⬜⬜ and ⬜

b. 16 ⬜⬜⬜ and ⬜

c. 18 ⬜⬜⬜ and ⬜

6. Find the prime factors of each number by completing the factor tree.

a. 16 — 2, ...

b. 8 — 2, ...

c. 28 — 2, ...

32

Number Patterns

1. Use a calculator to help you continue each number pattern.

	Rule	Pattern			
a.	x0.1	8385	838.5		
b.	x4	2	8		
c.	+150	265	415		
d.	-36	720	684		
e.	÷0.1	2	20		

2. Colour the multiples of 6 on this hundred chart.

1	2	3	4	5	6	7	8	9	1
11	12	13	14	15	16	17	18	19	2
21	22	23	24	25	26	27	28	29	3
31	32	33	34	35	36	37	38	39	4
41	42	43	44	45	46	47	48	49	5
51	52	53	54	55	56	57	58	59	6
61	62	63	64	65	66	67	68	69	7
71	72	73	74	75	76	77	78	79	8
81	82	83	84	85	86	87	88	89	9
91	92	93	94	95	96	97	98	99	10

3. Write the **triangular** numbers to 36.

4. Write the **square** numbers to 64.

5. Add consecutive, triangular numbers to reveal a pattern.

a. 10 and 15 _____ **b.** 28 and 36 _____

c. 21 and 28 _____ **d.** 45 and 55 _____

The additions result in a _____ number.

6. Write the **square** of each number.

a. $2^2 =$ _____ **b.** $6^2 =$ _____ **c.** $9^2 =$ _____

d. $7^2 =$ _____ **e.** $3^2 =$ _____ **f.** $5^2 =$ _____

Angles

Draw each angle.

a. Reflex   b. Right Angle   c. Obtuse Angle

Show each angle on a protractor.

a. 50°   b. 120°

c. 130°   d. 30°

 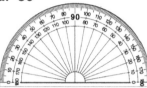

A straight angle equals 180°. Write the size of the other angle on the straight line.

a.

150°

= _____ °

b.

70°

= _____ °

c.

= _____ °

d.

110°

= _____ °

e.

133°

= _____ °

f.
145°

= _____ °

One revolution equals 360°. Find the size of the reflex angle.

a.

60°

= _____ °

b.
130°

= _____ °

c.
85°

= _____ °

a. The sum of three angles of a triangle equal

_____ °

b. The sum of the four angles of a quadrilateral is

_____ °

How many vertices in a triangle? [ ]

Circles

1. Match the distances on each circle to its name.

a.

b.

c.

d.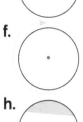

| radius |
| diameter |
| circumference |
| quadrant |
| semicircle |
| sector |
| arc |
| chord |

e.

f.

g.

h.

2. Find the size of the diameter or radius.

a.
10cm

radius

= _____

b.
4cm

diameter

= _____

c.
3.5cm

diameter

= _____

3. a. Half a circle is a _____.

b. A small section of a circle is an _____.

c. A chord does not pass through the _____.

d. If the radius is 9 cm the diameter is _____ cm.

e. All circles have a _____.

4. Use a pair of compasses to draw a circle with a diameter of 4 cm.

X centre

Money

1. Find the **discount** price of each item.

a. Reg. Price $12 Coffee 25% off   New Price

b. Reg. Price $2.40 50% off   New Price

c. Reg. Price $3.60 BUTTER 10% off   New Price

_____   _____   _____

d. Reg. Price $6 20% off   New Price

e. Reg. Price $5 Vanilla ice cream 25% off   New Price

f. Reg. Price $6.50 honey 30% off   New Price

_____   _____   _____

2. Write each as a percentage.

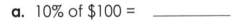

a. $0.3 =$ ____%   b. $\frac{1}{2} =$ ____%   c. $0.6 =$ ____%

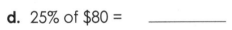

d. $\frac{1}{5} =$ ____%   e. $0.75 =$ ____%   f. $0.1 =$ ____%

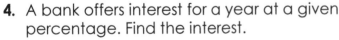

g. $\frac{1}{4} =$ ____%   h. $\frac{3}{10} =$ ____%   i. $0.8 =$ ____%

3. Find the percentage of each sum of money.

a. 10% of $100 = _____

b. 10% of $20 = _____

c. 25% of $200 = _____

d. 25% of $80 = _____

e. 50% of $150 = _____

f. 50% of $30 = _____

4. A bank offers interest for a year at a given percentage. Find the interest.

a. Banked $200 @ 5% interest _____

b. Banked $200 @ 10% interest _____

c. Banked $200 @ 3% interest _____

d. Banked $200 @ 7% interest _____

5. Find the percentage of each whole number.

a. 25% of 600 = _____   b. 10% of 30 = _____

Fractions

1. Colour the given fraction in each shape

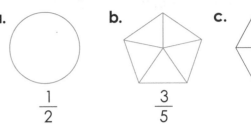

a. $\frac{1}{2}$ b. $\frac{3}{5}$ c. $\frac{5}{6}$

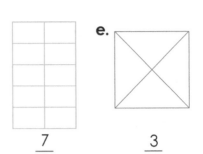

d. $\frac{7}{10}$ e. $\frac{3}{4}$ f. $\frac{3}{8}$

2. Write an equivalent fraction.

a. $\frac{1}{4} = \frac{\Box}{8}$ b. $\frac{3}{4} = \frac{\Box}{8}$ c. $\frac{2}{5} = \Box$

d. $\frac{3}{4} = \frac{\Box}{12}$ e. $\frac{2}{3} = \frac{\Box}{6}$ f. $\frac{4}{5} = \Box$

3. To add or subtract fractions the denominators MUST be the same. Add or subtract these fractions.

a. $\frac{2}{3} + \frac{1}{6} =$ b. $\frac{5}{8} + \frac{1}{4} =$ c. $\frac{3}{10} + \frac{2}{5} =$

$\boxed{} + \frac{1}{6} = \boxed{}$ $\frac{5}{8} + \boxed{} = \boxed{}$ $\frac{3}{10} + \boxed{} = $

d. $\frac{2}{3} - \frac{1}{6} =$ e. $\frac{7}{8} - \frac{3}{4} =$ f. $\frac{7}{10} - \frac{2}{5} =$

$\boxed{} - \frac{1}{6} = \boxed{}$ $\frac{7}{8} - \boxed{} = \boxed{}$ $\frac{7}{10} - \boxed{} = $

4. Complete the subtractions. Change the whole numbers to an equivalent fraction first.

a. $1 - \frac{1}{4} =$ b. $1 - \frac{2}{5} =$ c. $1 - \frac{3}{8} =$

$\boxed{} - \frac{1}{4} = \boxed{}$ $\boxed{} - \frac{2}{5} = \boxed{}$ $\boxed{} - \frac{3}{8} = $

Transformation

Reflect, **translate** or **rotate** each shape.

a. REFLECT

b. ROTATE

c. TRANSLATE

Use **reflection** to draw the other half of the numeral or letter.

a.    **b.**

c.   **d.**

Identify the transitions in each of the shapes.

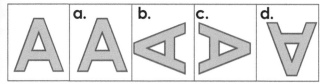

a. _____   **b.** _____

c. _____   **d.** _____

Use the tiles to rotate, reflect and translate to make a pattern.

 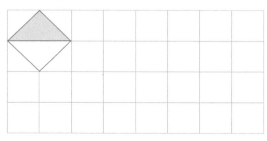

Chance

1. Roll the die 20 times. Record the results using tallies.

Tallies ____ ____ ____ ____ ____ ____

a. Which number turned up the **most**?____

b. What was the **difference** between the **most** and the **least** number turned up?

c. What was the combined total of **odd** numbers that turned up?

d. What was the percentage for each result? (Multiply each result by 5.)

____% ____% ____% ____% ____% ____%

2. Here is a spinner with 5 colours. Write the chance of each colour winning as a percentage?

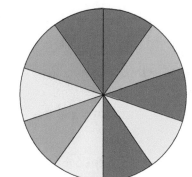

a. green _____ %

b. blue _____ %

c. yellow _____ %

d. purple _____ %

e. red _____ %

3. Use a standard pack of 52 cards to complete each experiment.

a. Write as a percentage, the chance of selecting a red card first draw. _____ %

b. Write as a percentage, the chance of selecting a heart first draw. _____ %

c. Write as a fraction, the chance of selecting a 7 first draw.

d. Record the number of cards drawn before drawing an Ace.

'A' tallies _____ Total _____

e. Repeat to draw a Queen.

'Q' tallies _____ Total _____ **35**

Order of Operations

1. Do the brackets first.

a. $7 + (5 - 2) =$ ☐
b. $5 \times (3 + 6) =$ ☐

c. $4 \times (3 - 1) =$ ☐
d. $(5 - 3) \times 6 =$ ☐

e. $(5 + 4) - 7 =$ ☐
f. $(6 + 1) - 3 =$ ☐

g. $5 \times (2 + 3) =$ ☐
h. $(7 + 3) \div 2 =$ ☐

2. Working from left to right, complete each number sentence. Remember the order of operations.

a. $13 + (6 \times 2) =$ ☐
b. $12 - (2 \times 4) =$ ☐

c. $14 - (3 \times 3) =$ ☐
d. $16 \div 4 + 3 =$ ☐

e. $15 \div 3 - 2 =$ ☐
f. $27 \div 3 + 2 =$ ☐

g. $51 \div 17 + 6 =$ ☐
h. $39 \div 13 + 8 =$ ☐

3. Complete these, still working from left to right.

a. $(17 + 1) \div 3 + 2 =$ ☐
b. $(16 - 3) \times 2 + 1 =$ ☐

c. $(12 + 4) \div 2 + 3 =$ ☐
d. $(8 + 3) - 4 \times 2 =$ ☐

e. $(5 + 7) - 3 \times 2 =$ ☐
f. $(7 + 9) \div 4 + 1 =$ ☐

g. $(7 \times 3) + (2 \times 4) =$ ☐
h. $(5 \times 2) - 6 + 1 =$ ☐

4. Complete each sentence. 'of' is done after the brackets.

a. $\frac{1}{2}$ of $(3 + 7) =$ ☐
b. $\frac{1}{4}$ of $(5 + 11) =$ ☐

c. $\frac{1}{5}$ of $(10 \times 2) =$ ☐
d. $\frac{1}{3}$ of $(7 \times 3) =$ ☐

e. $\frac{1}{10}$ of $(8 \times 5) =$ ☐
f. $\frac{1}{2}$ of $(72 - 24) =$ ☐

5. Varying the brackets give different answers.

a. $6 \times 2 + 3 \times 4 =$ ☐
b. $6 \times (2 + 3) \times 4 =$ ☐

c. $(6 \times 2 + 3) \times 4 =$ ☐

Decimal Fractions

1. Write the proper fraction for each decim

a. $0.25 =$ ☐
b. $0.75 =$ ☐
c. $0.7 =$

d. $0.5 =$ ☐
e. $0.125 =$ ☐
f. $0.4 =$

g. $0.666 =$ ☐
h. $0.2 =$ ☐
i. $0.8 =$

j. $0.333 =$ ☐
k. $0.875 =$ ☐
l. $0.6 =$

2. Write the place value for each circled number.

a. $0.\textcircled{3}52$ _____
b. $\textcircled{1}.354$ _____

c. $1.3\textcircled{3}6$ _____
d. $2.\textcircled{7}0$ _____

e. $\textcircled{2}2.53$ _____
f. $0.33\textcircled{1}$ _____

3. Join the decimal fraction to its place on the number line.

0

4. Multiply each fraction by 100.

a. 0.032 _____
b. 1.750 _____

c. 2.356 _____
d. 7.358 _____

e. 14.32 _____
f. 0.01 _____

5. Add the missing decimal fraction between each of these.

a. 0.5 _____ 0.4
b. 0.7 _____ 0.8

c. 2.6 _____ 2.7
d. 1.3 _____ 2.3

e. 0.75 _____ 0.85
f. 0.22 _____ 0.24

Area

What is the area of a rectangle with these sides?

a. Length 8cm
Width 4cm

Area = ☐ cm²

b. Length 4cm
Width 3cm

Area = ☐ cm²

c. Length 9cm
Width 2cm

Area = ☐ cm²

d. Length 10cm
Width 2.5cm

Area = ☐ cm²

Find the area of each rectangle.
Not to scale.

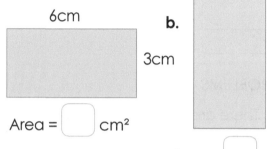

a. 6cm
3cm

Area = ☐ cm²

b. 3cm
7cm

Area = ☐ cm²

c. 11cm
4cm

Area = ☐ cm²

Find the length of the side for each rectangle.

a. Width is 4cm, area is 32 cm² ☐ cm

b. Area 48cm², width 12cm ☐ cm

c. Area 27cm², width 3cm ☐ cm

Find the area of each triangle.
Remember: half the base times heigh

a. Area = ☐ cm²   **b.** Area = ☐ cm²

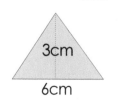

4cm

4cm

3cm

6cm

Line Graph

This line graph shows two cars travelling for 5 hours. Use the information to complete the questions.

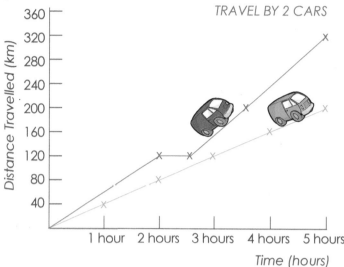

TRAVEL BY 2 CARS

Distance Travelled (km)

360 320 280 240 200 160 120 80 40

1 hour 2 hours 3 hours 4 hours 5 hours

Time (hours)

1. How far did the blue car travel in 3 hours? _____

2. How long did it take the blue car to travel 100 kilometres? _____

3. At what speed did the blue car travel over 3 hours? _____

4. How long did it take the blue car to travel 160 kilometres? _____

5. How far would the blue car travel in 6 hours at the same speed? _____

6. How far did the red car travel before it stopped for a break? _____

7. How long was its break? _____

8. At what speed did the red car travel before it stopped for a break? _____

9. After the break, the red car increased its speed to _____

10. After 2 hours, how much further had the red car travelled than the blue car? _____

11. How much further than the blue car did the red car travel in the 5 hours? _____

37

Integers

Two-digit Multiplication

1. Show each number sentence on the number line. Write the result.

a. $-3 + 2 - 6 + 5 - 1 =$ ⬚

0

b. $-4 + 5 + 4 - 3 =$ ⬚

0

c. $+3 - 7 - 2 + 3 - 4 =$ ⬚

0

d. $-5 - 3 + 6 - 4 + 1 =$ ⬚

0

2. Write each group of numbers in **ascending** order.

a. -2, +3, -5, -3, +2, 0, -4, +4

_____

b. +6, -4, +2, +3, -3, -2, 0, +1

_____

c. -0.2, +0.1, +0.5, -0.3, 0, -0.1, +0.3

_____

d. -100, +200, -50, 0 +150, -200, +50

_____

3. Complete each number sentence. Some will have negative answers.

a. $+3 - 7 =$ ⬚   b. $-5 + 9 =$ ⬚

c. $-6 + 4 =$ ⬚   d. $+8 - 12 =$ ⬚

e. $+7 - 14 =$ ⬚   f. $-9 + 3 =$ ⬚

38

1. Find the product of each algorithm. Use the extended form of multiplication One is done for you.

a.
```
    6 2 3
  x   2 7
    +1 +2
  4 3 6 1
+ 1 2 4 6 0   Add
            a zero
  1 6 8 2 1
```

b.
```
    3 2 5
  x   3 5
```

c.
```
      4
    x
```

d.
```
    6 3 5
  x   4 6
```

e.
```
    4 1 5
  x   3 8
```

f.
```
      6
    x
```

2. PROBLEMS

a. There are 64 pieces of liquorice in a bag. How many pieces in 37 bags?

_____
x _____

_____
_____ pieces

b. 48 rows seat 52 people in a mov theatre. How many seats in th theatre?

_____
x _____

_____
_____ se

3. Find the product of each four-digit multiplication. Use the extended form.

a.
```
  3 2 4 1
x     3 7
```

b.
```
  5 2 1 6
x     4 9
```

c.
```
  3 7 2
x     2
```

d.
```
  8 3 5 8
x     6 4
```

e.
```
  4 3 1 9
x     2 3
```

f.
```
  6 2 1
x     4
```

Volume

d the volume of each container.

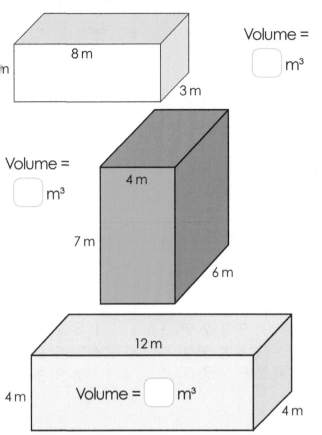

Volume =
☐ m³

Volume =
☐ m³

Volume = ☐ m³

d the length of the unknown side using the
en dimensions.

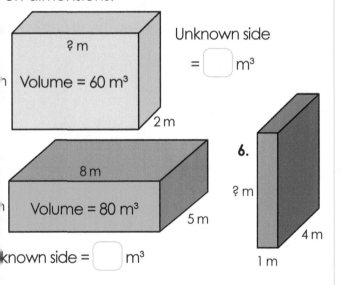

Unknown side
= ☐ m³

6.

known side = ☐ m³

Volume = 24 m³

Unknown side = ☐ m³

Write the capacity for boxes with these
specific dimensions.

a. Length 6cm, width 7cm,
   height 4cm =   _____ cm³

b. Length 8cm, width 4cm,
   height 6cm =   _____ cm³

c. Length 4cm, width 5cm,
   height 3cm =   _____ cm³

Cartesian Co-ordinates

1. Plot each set of co-ordinates on the graph.
   Draw an 'X' at each point.

   a. (+ 2 - 3), (- 3 + 2)   b. (+ 3 + 2), (- 3 - 1)

   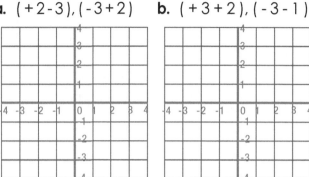

   c. (- 2, - 3), (+ 3 - 1)   d. (- 3, +3), (+ 2 - 3)

   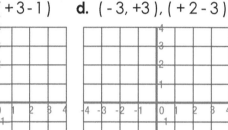

   e. (+ 2, + 3), (- 3, -3)   f. (+2, -2), (-1, + 4)

   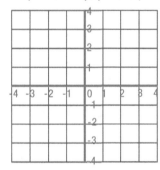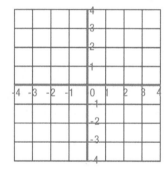

2. Write the co-ordinates for each letter
   showing on the grid.

   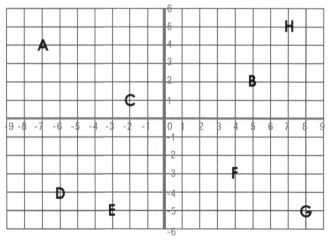

   A = _____   B = _____   C = _____

   D = _____   E = _____   F = _____

   G = _____   H = _____

Place Value

1. Write the number showing on the abacus by the counters.

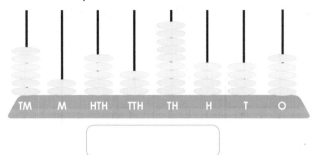

| TM | M | HTH | TTH | TH | H | T | O |

[ ]

2. Arrange 4,9,6,3,2,8,7,1,4 to make the **largest** possible number.

[ ]

3. How many millions in 48 326 172? [ ]

4. Round off 38 716 214 to the nearest million. [ ]

5. 30 000 000 + 8 000 000 + 200 000 + 40 000 + 7 000 + 900 + 60 + 4 =

[ ]

Arrange each set of numbers in **ascending** order

6. 38 217 430, 18 516 210, 49 324 788, 23 417 602

_____

7. 72 517 930, 48 612 622, 59 384 517, 90 813 210

_____

8. 62 517 311, 43 290 857, 49 853 729, 30 217 643

_____

9. How many ten thousands in 48 362 711? [ ]

10. 100 000 **more** than 29 362 780. [ ]

11. Round off the numbers to the **nearest** million.

a. 47 563 727 _____

b. 3 953 162 _____

c. 24 762 385 _____

Addition

1. Find the total for each algorithm.

a.

TTH	TH	H	T	U
8	3	6	4	1
	3	2	8	7
+		5	1	0	2

b.

TTH	TH	H	T	U
1	5	3	2	7
3	2	8	9	1
+			4	3	8

c.

TTH	TH	H	T	U
5	4	3	0	4
	3	2	8	4
+	2	8	5	6

d.

TTH	TH	H	T	U
6	4	1	3	2
2	8	4	1	3
+	2	8	5	4

e.

TTH	TH	H	T	U
	9	3	2	7
3	4	5	3	3
+ 2	8	9	7	3

f.

TTH	TH	H	T	U
1	3	2	8	7
4	1	5	6	2
+	2	8	3	3

2. The attendance at the five day cricket match was 42 327 on day 1, 33 265 day 2, 25 169 day 3, 31 565 day 4 and 12 250 on the last day. How many attended the match in total?

3. Add each sum of money.

a. $2713.54
   1690.38
+2683.09
$.

b. $4712.55
   2007.93
+6985.02
$.

4. Use a calculator to add the group of numbers.

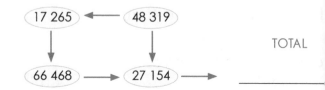

| 17 265 | ← | 48 319 |

TOTAL

| 66 468 | → | 27 154 | → |

3D Objects

Name the 3D objects made by each net.

a.

b.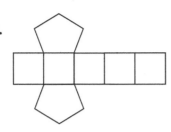

_____   _____

c.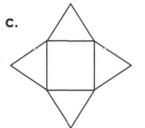

d.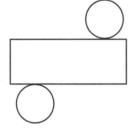

_____   _____

e.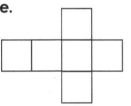

f.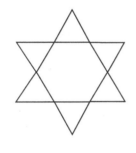

_____   _____

Name each 3D object drawn from these various views.

a.

b.

_____   _____

c.

d.

_____   _____

e.

f.

_____   _____

Possibilities

1. Here is a menu that shows two entrees, two main meals and two desserts. Complete the tree diagram to show the possible combinations.

 My Place the Palace

Entree: Soup of the Day (S)
Mini Pizza (P)

Mains: Fish, Chips and Salad (F)
Beef with Chips and Salad (B)

Desserts: Three Flavour Icecreams (I)
Cheese Cake (C)

TREE DIAGRAM
DINNER

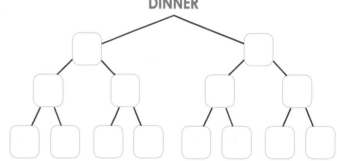

2. How many different combinations are possible for two people? _____

3. If each meal cost $12, what would it cost for four people to have all three courses? _____

4. Here are four spinners. Write the chance, as a percentage, for each one to fall on yellow.

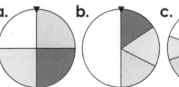

_____ %   _____ %   _____ %   _____ %

5. Write each outcome as a fraction.

a. Landing a die on an even number. ☐

b. Rolling a six on a die.

41

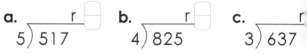

Money

1. Write the discounted price for each item.

a.  $890 less 10%

Discount price _____

b. $480 less 25%

Discount price _____

c.  $36 less 25%

Discount price _____

d.  $42 less 50%

Discount price _____

2. Write the percentage of each sum of money.

a. 25% of $200 = $ _____

b. 10% of $40 = $ _____

c. 50% of $600 = $ _____

d. 40% of $300 = $ _____

e. 30% of $240 = $ _____

3. Find the price of each item without GST. Remember to divide by 10 to get GST.

a.

$330 incl. GST

GST = $ _____

b.

$880 incl. GST

GST = $ _____

c.

$220 incl. GST

GST = $ _____

d.

$44 incl. GST

GST = $ _____

4. Jon wanted to buy a surf board. The tagged price showed $870 + GST. What was the price of the surf board with GST? $ _____

Division

1. Complete each division. Write the remainder as a fraction.

a. $5\overline{)517}$ r ☐

b. $4\overline{)825}$ r ☐

c. $3\overline{)637}$ r

d. $7\overline{)841}$ r ☐

e. $2\overline{)735}$ r ☐

f. $6\overline{)715}$ r

2. a. If I earn $180 in 6 hours how much do I earn per hour? $ _____

b. Joshua rides 210 kilometres each week. How far does he ride each day?   _____

c. If 936 cattle were branded in 3 hours, on average, how many are branded each hour?   _____

d. If a milkman delivers 840 cartons of milk in 4 days, how many does he deliver each day?   _____

3. Complete each division. Write the remainder as a decimal.

a. $4\overline{)2353.0}$

b. $5\overline{)5372.0}$

c. $2\overline{)3751.0}$

d. $10\overline{)3052.0}$

e. $4\overline{)8375.0}$

f. $2\overline{)7351.0}$

4. Divide each number by 10 or 100.

a. $374.24 \div 10 =$ _____

b. $451.6 \div 10 =$ _____

c. $351.1 \div 100 =$ _____

d. $83.2 \div 100 =$ _____

Angles

Calculate the size of the other angle.

a.

0 = _____°

b.

0 = _____°

c.

0 = _____°

d.

0 = _____°

e.

0 = _____°

f.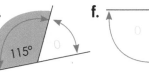

0 = _____°

The three angles of a triangle add to 180°. Find the size of the other angle in each triangle.

a.

z = _____°

b.

z = _____°

c.

z = _____°

d.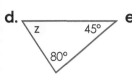

z = _____°

e.

z = _____°

f.

z = _____°

With lines that cross, opposite angles are equal. Find the size of the other angles.

a.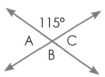

A = _____°

B = _____°

C = _____°

b.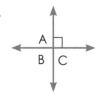

A = _____°

B = _____°

C = _____°

Find the size of each **reflex** angle.

a.

R = _____°

b.

R = _____°

c.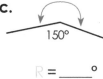

R = _____°

Time

1. Write the pm time on each clock face in 24 hour time.

a.

b.

c.

2. Write the 24 hour time in am or pm time.

a. 2345 = _____   **b.** 0730 = _____

c. 2136 = _____   **d.** 1550 = _____

e. 1748 = _____   **f.** 1936 = _____

g. 2017 = _____   **h.** 1445 = _____

3. Calculate the time lapse between each given time.

a. 0715 till 3:50pm _____

b. 1345 till 1837 _____

c. 8:30am Tuesday till
1325 the next day _____

d. 1351 8th August till
23:09 on 10th August _____

e. 1157 5th September till
0645 on 7th September _____

4. If you leave home at 8:15 am and arrive at your destination at 16:27,
how long was your journey? _____

5. Harry began his trip at 6:35 am and arrived 2 days later at 6:07 am.
How long was his journey? _____

6. How many days in 84 hours? _____

7. How many hours in 2 weeks? _____

43

Factors

1. Write either 'prime' or 'composite' for each number.

a. 7 _____ **b.** 9 _____

c. 8 _____ **d.** 11 _____

e. 21 _____ **f.** 23 _____

g. 39 _____ **h.** 51 _____

i. 67 _____ **j.** 73 _____

2. Circle the numbers that can be divided by each factor.

a. 2   7 , 9 , 4 , 12, 27, 34

b. 3   7 , 9 , 4 , 12, 27, 34

c. 5   6 , 10, 17, 25, 38, 75

3. Write the prime factors for these.

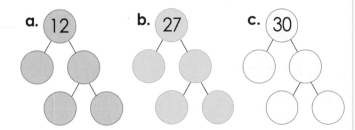

a. 12   **b.** 27   **c.** 30

4. Write the factors for each number.

a. 12

b. 16

c. 28

5. Write the factors for each number.
Write whether prime (P) or composite (C).

a. 8 _____ ( )   **b.** 9 _____ ( )

c. 11 _____ ( )   **d.** 19 _____ ( )

e. 6 _____ ( )   **f.** 17 _____ ( )

Fractions

1. Write each fraction in its lowest form.

a. $\frac{14}{21} =$ **b.** $\frac{8}{12} =$ **c.** $\frac{9}{27} =$

d. $\frac{8}{10} =$ **e.** $\frac{6}{10} =$ **f.** $\frac{10}{20} =$

g. $\frac{9}{12} =$ **h.** $\frac{2}{8} =$ **i.** $\frac{4}{20} =$

2. Change the improper fraction to a mixed number fraction. Divide the denominator into the numerator.

$\frac{8}{5} = 1\frac{3}{5}$ **a.** $\frac{11}{5} =$ _____   **b.** $\frac{11}{8} =$ _____

c. $\frac{5}{2} =$ _____   **d.** $\frac{9}{7} =$ _____   **e.** $\frac{5}{4} =$ _____

f. $\frac{12}{5} =$ _____   **g.** $\frac{7}{3} =$ _____   **h.** $\frac{12}{10} =$ _____

3. Write each fraction as a percentage.

a. $\frac{1}{5} =$ _____%   **b.** $\frac{3}{4} =$ _____%   **c.** $\frac{3}{10} =$ _____

d. $\frac{1}{2} =$ _____%   **e.** $\frac{4}{5} =$ _____%   **f.** $\frac{1}{4} =$ _____

4. Write each fraction as a decimal fraction.

a. $\frac{1}{2} =$ _____   **b.** $\frac{1}{4} =$ _____   **c.** $\frac{2}{5} =$ _____

d. $\frac{3}{4} =$ _____   **e.** $\frac{4}{5} =$ _____   **f.** $\frac{8}{10} =$ _____

5. Round off each number to two decimal places.

a. 1.738 _____   **b.** 2.654 _____

c. 4.175 _____   **d.** 1.516 _____

Diagonals

Cartesian Plane

Draw and then count the number of diagonals in each shape.

a.

[ ] diagonals

b.

[ ] diagonals

c.

[ ] diagonals

d.

[ ] diagonals

Colour the shapes that have **no** diagonals.

a.

b.

c.

d.

e.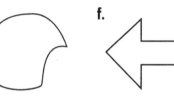

f.

Write the number of sides, angles and diagonals in each shape.

a.

[ ] sides [ ] angles

[ ] diagonals

b.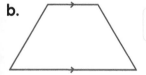

[ ] sides [ ] angles

[ ] diagonals

c.

[ ] sides [ ] angles

[ ] diagonals

d.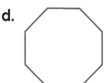

[ ] sides [ ] angles

[ ] diagonals

1. Plot the points identified in each set of co-ordinates.

a. (4, -2), (-3, 2)

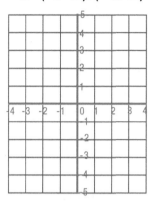

b. (3, 4), (-2, -4)

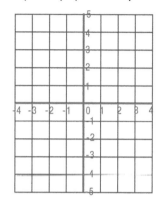

c. (2, 4), (-3, -4)

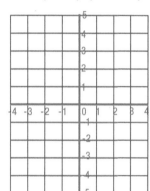

d. (-3, 5), (3, -4)

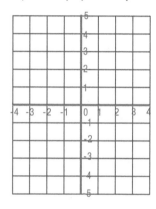

2. Write the co-ordinates for each shape or symbol on the Cartesian plane.

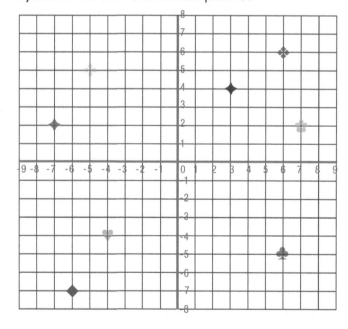

a. ✤ = _____

b. ❖ = _____

c. ✦ = _____

d. ✦ = _____

e. ✿ = _____

f. ♥ = _____

g. ◆ = _____

h. ♣ = _____

45

Square and Triangular Numbers

1. Draw a line to match each digit squared to its squared number.

2^2 3^2 4^2 5^2 6^2 7^2

(25) (16) (9) (49) (4) (36)

2. Write the square number for each one.

a. $8^2 =$ _____ **b.** $9^2 =$ _____ **c.** $10^2 =$ _____

d. $4^2 =$ _____ **e.** $12^2 =$ _____ **f.** $11^2 =$ _____

3. Add each set of square numbers.

a. $3^2 + 7^2 =$ ☐   **b.** $5^2 + 4^2 =$ ☐

☐ + ☐ = ☐   ☐ + ☐ = ☐

c. $6^2 + 2^2 =$ ☐   **d.** $3^2 + 8^2 =$ ☐

☐ + ☐ = ☐   ☐ + ☐ = ☐

4. Write the triangular number for each group of counters.

a.
b.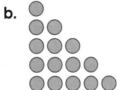
c.

☐   ☐   ☐

5. Add consecutive numbers to find the triangular number.

a. 1 + 2 + 3 + 4 + 5 + 6 + 7 = ☐

b. 1 + 2 + 3 + 4 + 5 = ☐

c. 1 + 2 + 3 + 4 + 5 + 6 + 7 + 8 = ☐

6. Fill in the table of missing triangular numbers.

1	3		10	
21	28		45	

46

Number Patterns

1. Fill in the missing numbers in each group. Look for the pattern.

a.

7	11	13	17			

b.

4	9	16	25			

c.

1	3	6	10			

2. Apply the rule in the centre to the adjacent number and finish the number wheels.

a.

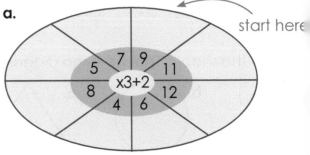

start here

7 9
5   11
×3+2
8   12
4 6

b.

start here

40 72
24   36
÷4+3
48   64
32 16

3. Add the consecutive, triangular number to find a square number.

a. 6 + 10 = ☐   **b.** 15 + 21 = ☐

c. 10 + 15 = ☐   **d.** 36 + 45 = ☐

e. 21 + 28 = ☐   **f.** 45 + 55 = ☐

4. Continue each number pattern.

Rule	Pattern
× 2 + 4	17, 38, ____, ____, ____
× 3 - 5	5, 10, ____, ____, ____
× 0.1	9000, 900, ____, ____, ____
× 10	7, 70, ____, ____, ____

Length

Use a ruler to draw a line the given length.

a. 67mm •

b. 35mm •

c. 18mm •

d. 51mm •

Measure the length of each line in millimetres.

a. _____ ⬜

b. _____ ⬜ mm

mm

c. _____ ⬜ mm

Write each measurement in metres using decimal notation.

a. 1536 mm ⬜ m   **b.** 8273 mm ⬜ m

c. 85 mm ⬜ m   **d.** 756 mm ⬜ m

e. 986 mm ⬜ m   **f.** 1360 mm ⬜ m

Use a ruler to measure the perimeter of each 2D shape to the nearest millimetre.

a.   **b.**

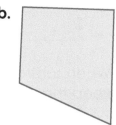

c.   **d.**

Use the scale 1 cm = 3 km to find the perimeter of each shape.

a. 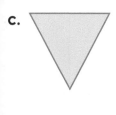 $2\frac{1}{2}$cm   **b.**

cm

3cm   2cm

6cm

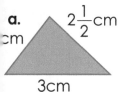
erimeter = _____km   perimeter = _____km

Data Combinations

1. Here is a graph of student heights. Read the graph and then complete the questions.

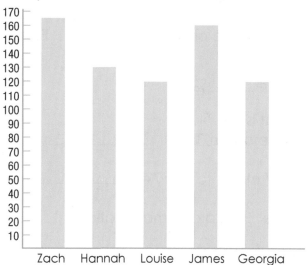

a. How tall is Georgia? _____ cm

b. What is the difference in height between Zach and Louise? _____ cm

c. How much taller is James than Georgia? _____ cm

d. What is the average height of the boys? _____ cm

e. What is the average height of the girls? _____ cm

f. Calculate the average height of the students. _____ cm

2. Sometimes data does not give a true picture of a larger issue. Circle either '**credible**' or '**misleading**' for each statement.

a. The average height of Year 6 students in the Nation's schools is 140 cm.

credible   **misleading**

b. Ten students were surveyed and the results show 9 out of 10 students like to eat pies for lunch.

credible   **misleading**

c. Twenty people were surveyed about the type of car they drive. The results showed 75% of people owned a Holden. 75% of Australians drive a Holden.

credible   **misleading**

47

Decimal Fractions

1. 0.85 to the nearest tenth _____

2. 867.2 - 538.4 = _____

3. $\frac{4}{5}$ = 0.4 True or False? True ☐ False ☐

4. $\frac{87}{100}$ = _____ %

5. What is the place value of 7 in 3.87? _____

6. Is 6.7 closer to 6 or 7? _____

7. Write $\frac{3}{5}$ as a decimal fraction. _____

8. Write 35% as a decimal fraction. _____

9. Write $\frac{3}{4}$ as a percentage. _____

10. 20% of $800 = $ _____

11. Remove the non-significant zeros from each number. Re-write the decimal.

   a. 0.320   b. 0.740   c. 3.720

   _____   _____   _____

   d. 0.1070   e. 70.450   f. 02.020

   _____   _____   _____

12. Show each fraction as a decimal.

   a.   b.   c.

   _____   _____   _____

13. Write each fraction as a decimal.

   a. $\frac{1}{4}$ = _____   b. $\frac{2}{5}$ = _____   c. $\frac{7}{10}$ = _____

   d. $\frac{3}{4}$ = _____   e. $\frac{1}{2}$ = _____   f. $\frac{6}{8}$ = _____

14. Write each decimal as a fraction.

   a. 0.6 = ☐   b. 0.125 = ☐

   c. 0.333 = ☐   d. 0.875 = ☐

Working with Decimals

1. Add the decimals. Remember to keep the decimal points aligned (under each other).

   a. 83.72   b. 435.22   c. 382.?
      +17.64   +176.89   +453.?
   _____.   _____.   _____.

   d. 623.33   e. 335.16   f. 671.?
      127.84   273.84   247.?
     +215.55   +129.86   +167.?
   _____.   _____.   _____.

2. Add each sum of money. Remember to keep correct place value for cents and dollars.

   a. $3287.65   b. $2561.75
         462.36   3820.72
       +1285.99   +3179.06
   $_____. $_____.

   c. $6348.56   d. $3725.86
         217.77   873.94
       +   80.56   +2685.79
   $_____. $_____.

3. When subtracting decimals remember to keep the decimal points aligned.

   a. 372.16   b. 336.27   c. 485.1?
     -157.29   -107.19   - 99.8?
   _____.   _____.   _____.

4. Paris' mother had $160 to spend at the supermarket. Add the cost of goods and then calculate her change.

Vegemite $6.32	Change
Cereal $5.97	$160.0?
Milk $3.95	
Bread $4.64	Spend.....
	_____
Spent.................... $ _____	Change $ _____

Mass

Colour the items measured in **tonnes**.

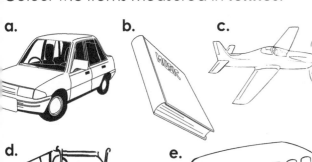

a.   b.   c.

d.   e.

Write the kilograms in tonnes in decimal notation. One is done for you.

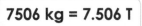

7506 kg = 7.506 T	**a.** 3655kg = _____

b. 3252kg = _____   **c.** 2587kg = _____

d. 1740kg = _____   **e.** 785kg = _____

f. 2726kg = _____   **g.** 75kg = _____

Write each tonnage as kilograms.

a. 6 tonnes = _____ kg

b. $7\frac{1}{2}$ tonnes = _____kg

c. $3\frac{1}{4}$ tonnes = _____kg

d. $4\frac{3}{4}$ tonnes = _____ kg

e. 2.05 tonnes = _____ kg

f. 16 tonnes = _____ kg

Write the unit of mass for each object; grams (g), kilograms (kg) tonnes (T).

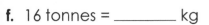

a.   **b.**   **c.**

30 ☐   36 ☐   7 ☐

d.   **e.**   **f.**

300 ☐   75 ☐   3 ☐

Data/Time

1. Calculate the difference showing between the two odometers and write the distance travelled.

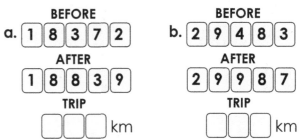

BEFORE   **BEFORE**

a. 1 8 3 7 2   **b.** 2 9 4 8 3

AFTER   **AFTER**

1 8 8 3 9   2 9 9 8 7

TRIP   **TRIP**

☐☐☐ km   ☐☐☐ km

2. Write the speed showing on each odometer.

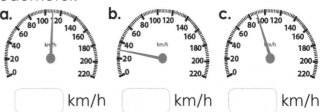

a.   **b.**   **c.**

☐ km/h   ☐ km/h   ☐ km/h

3. Show the speed each car needs to travel to achieve the given time.

  a. 140 kilometres   **b.** 250 kilometres
     in 2 hours   in 5 hours

4. Use the line graph to complete the activities.

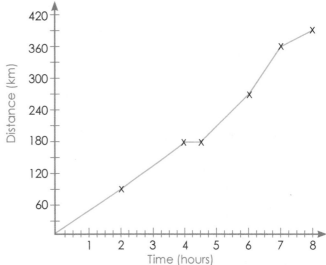

a. How long did it take
    to travel 120 km?   _____

b. At what distance was
    the first break taken? _____

c. How long was that break? _____

d. How far was travelled in 8 hours? _____ **49**

Averages

1. Find the average height, mass or length of each group of people, goods and fish.

a.

1.83m   1.68m   1.53m

Family's average height

☐ m

b.

4.3kg   3.2kg   4.5kg

Average mass

☐ kg

c.

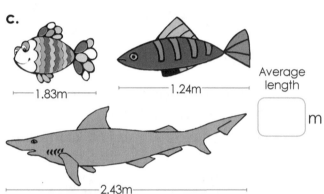

├── 1.83m ──┤   ├──── 1.24m ────┤

├──────── 2.43m ────────┤

Average length

☐ m

2. Find the average.

a. Sam's class results were 64 for English, 78 for Maths, 72 for Science, 86 for P.E. and 74 for History. What was his average mark? He needs 75 or more to go to University.

Average mark _____

University ☐ Yes ☐ No

b. A car travels 240 kilometres in 3 hours. What was its average speed per hour

_____ km/h

3. Find the average for each group of numbers.

a. 3616, 2515 and 7258 _____

b. 7.24, 3.86, 5.15, 6.75, 2.15 _____

c. $72.55, $38.60, $53.52 $ _____

d. $\frac{3}{5}, \frac{1}{4}, \frac{3}{4}$ ☐   **e.** $\frac{1}{2}, \frac{1}{5}, \frac{4}{5}$ ☐

50

Improper Fractions

1. Change the improper fractions to a mixed numeral.

a. $\frac{8}{5} =$ ___   **b.** $\frac{5}{2} =$ ___   **c.** $\frac{5}{3} =$ ___

d. $\frac{13}{8} =$ ___   **e.** $\frac{7}{4} =$ ___   **f.** $\frac{12}{5} =$ ___

g. $\frac{11}{3} =$ ___   **h.** $\frac{11}{5} =$ ___   **i.** $\frac{8}{3} =$ ___

2. Add the fractions. Write the mixed nume

a. $\frac{7}{8} + \frac{7}{8} =$ ☐ ___   **b.** $\frac{4}{5} + \frac{4}{5} =$ ☐ ___

c. $\frac{5}{8} + \frac{7}{8} =$ ☐ ___   **d.** $\frac{5}{6} + \frac{3}{6} =$ ☐ ___

e. $\frac{2}{5} + \frac{4}{5} =$ ☐ ___   **f.** $\frac{7}{10} + \frac{5}{10} =$ ☐ ___

3. Add each fraction. Find the lowest, common denominator first. Change improper fractions to mixed numerals.

a. $\frac{3}{4} + \frac{1}{2} =$ ___
$\frac{3}{4} +$ ☐ $=$ ☐

b. $\frac{3}{4} + \frac{5}{8} =$ ___
☐ $+ \frac{5}{8} =$ ☐

c. $\frac{5}{8} + \frac{1}{2} =$ ___
$\frac{5}{8} +$ ☐ $=$ ☐

d. $\frac{3}{4} + \frac{7}{8} =$ ___
☐ $+ \frac{7}{8} =$ ☐

e. $\frac{4}{5} + \frac{7}{10} =$ ___
☐ $+ \frac{7}{10} =$ ☐

f. $\frac{9}{10} + \frac{2}{5} =$ ___
$\frac{9}{10} +$ ☐ $=$ ☐

4. Change each mixed numeral to an improper fraction.

a. $1\frac{1}{2} =$ ☐   **b.** $2\frac{1}{4} =$ ☐   **c.** $1\frac{3}{4} =$ ☐

d. $1\frac{5}{8} =$ ☐   **e.** $4\frac{1}{2} =$ ☐   **f.** $1\frac{1}{3} =$ ☐

Volume and Capacity

Probability and Combinations

Write the mass and volume of each measure of water.

a. 500mL **b.** 750mL **c.** 2150mL

_____ g   _____ g   _____ g

_____ cm³   _____ cm³   _____ cm³

Add the correct unit of measurement for each container. (L, mL, g, kg, cm³, m³)

a.

b.

c.

3000 _____   390 _____   250 _____

d.

e.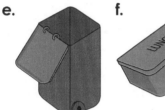

f.

8 _____   960 _____   400 _____

A container shows a water level of 500 mL. If an object is placed in the water and the new level in the container is now 750 mL how much water is displaced?   _____

Here are containers with items added. Record the displacement and mass in each one.

a. BEFORE   AFTER

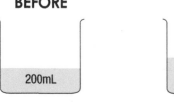

100mL

275mL

displacement _____   mass _____

b. BEFORE   AFTER

200mL

400mL

displacement _____   mass _____

1. Use the word bank to help label the scale of probability.

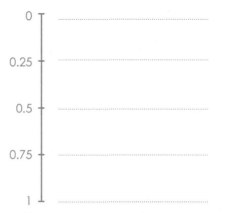

0
0.25
0.5
0.75
1

Word Bank

possible

certain

impossible

unlikely

50-50

2. Using the numbered scale, write as a number, the probability of each event occurring.

a. The next baby born will be a boy _____

b. I can read a novel in an hour. _____

c. My mum is a good cook. _____

d. Tomorrow will be sunny. _____

e. Pigs can fly backwards. _____

3. Write a word for each possibility.

a. I can throw a 7 with a die. _____

b. I can toss a head with a coin first go. _____

c. Christmas is in July. _____

d. Mid-winter is July. _____

4. Answer the questions below and complete the diagram.

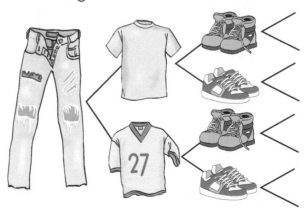

a. How many different combinations of clothing are possible? ☐

b. Add two belts to the clothing to extend the diagram. Now how many combinations of clothing? ☐

Money

1. Calculate the discount amount for each sum of money.

a. 10% of $600 _____ **b.** 10% of $750 _____

c. 10% of $350 _____ **d.** 25% of $800 _____

e. 25% of $240 _____ **f.** 25% of $720 _____

g. 50% of $950 _____ **h.** 50% of $1240 _____

2. Find the discount price for each item.

a.  $80 less 20%

b. $39 less 10%

c.  $60 less 25%

Discount Price   Discount Price   Discount Price

$ _____ $ _____ $ _____

3. PROBLEMS

a. What is the total interest charged on a loan of $2 400 at 10% for one year? _____

b. A car was priced at $22 750. If the buyer received 10% off, what did the buyer pay for the car? _____

4. Price each item after GST is added.

a.

b.

$19 750 + gst $75 750 + gst

Full price $ _____   Full price $ _____

5. Tick the items that attract a GST.

a.

b. Margarine Margarine

c.  milk 2L

d.

e.  BISCUITS

Multiplication

1. Find the product for each algorithm.

a. 793
  x   4
  _____

b. 836
  x   5
  _____

c. 728
  x   3
  _____

d. 586
  x   7
  _____

e. 368
  x   6
  _____

f. 496
  x   2
  _____

2. Use the extended form to find the product of each four-digit algorithm multiplied by a two-digit number.

a. 3724
  x   23

b. 5815
  x   34

c. 1362
  x   25

d. 5164
  x   38

e. 6125
  x   27

f. 4153
  x   46

3. PROBLEMS

$ _____

a. Dallas is saving $536 each week. How much will he save in one year? $ _____

b. Dad travels 127 km to work each day. How far does he travel in a fortnight? _____ X _____ k _____

c. The large stand at the footy stadium has 232 seats in each row. If there are 55 rows, how many seats are in the stand? _____ X _____ k _____

Angles

Write the size of the other angle or angles.

a. 70°

Z = _____°

b. 115° Z

Z = _____°

c. 50° Z

Z = _____°

d. 80° Z

Z = _____°

e. 45° Z

Z = _____°

f. Z 125°

Z = _____°

g. 135° X Y Z

X = _____°
Y = _____°
Z = _____°

h. X 75° Y Z

X = _____°
Y = _____°
Z = _____°

i. Y X 130° Z

X = _____°
Y = _____°
Z = _____°

Find the size of the other angle in each triangle.

a. 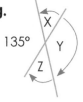 80° Z 45°

Z = _____°

b. Z 60°

Z = _____°

c. 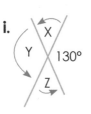 Z 110° 25°

Z = _____°

Find the size of the other angles in each quadrilateral.

a.  Z

Z = _____°

b. 115° Z

Z = _____°

c. 110° 112° Z 70°

Z = _____°

d. 120° Z 0° 60°

Z = _____°

e. 120° 110° Z 85°

Z = _____°

f. 115° Z 70°

Z = _____°

Location

1. Label the points of the directional rose.
   NB. The position of NE.

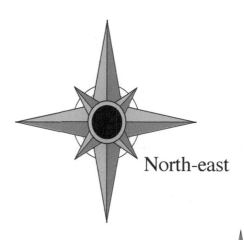

North-east

2. Write the direction for each piece of fruit in relation to the bowl.

 N

a.

b.

c.

d.

FRUIT BOWL

e.

f.

g.

h.

3. Plot the points and then join the dots to discover a 2D shape. Label each shape.

a. (3,3) (-3,3) (-2,-3) (2,-3) **b.** (3,2) (-2,2) (-3,-3) (2,-3)

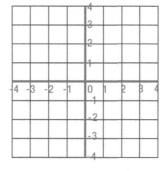

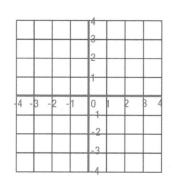

_____ _____

Integers

1. Fill in the number sentence as shown on each number line.

a.

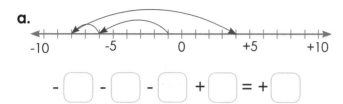

- ⬚ - ⬚ - ⬚ + ⬚ = + ⬚

b.

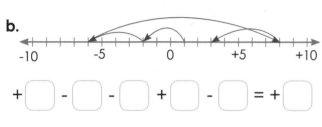

+ ⬚ - ⬚ - ⬚ + ⬚ - ⬚ = + ⬚

c.

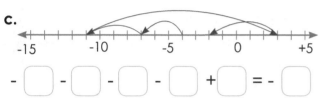

- ⬚ - ⬚ - ⬚ - ⬚ + ⬚ = - ⬚

2. Write the co-ordinates for each symbol.

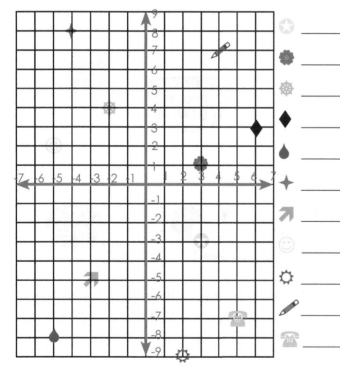

☆ _____
✿ _____
✵ _____
◆ _____
⬤ _____
✦ _____
↗ _____
☺ _____
✿ _____
✎ _____
☎ _____

3. Find the missing number to complete each sentence.

a. - 7 + ⬚ = - 2   **b.** + 8 - ⬚ = - 3

c. - 9 + ⬚ = -1   **d.** - 6 + ⬚ = - 4

e. + 3 - ⬚ = - 7   **f.** - ⬚ - 4 = - 7

g. - ⬚ + 5 = - 3   **h.** + 6 - ⬚ = - 5

Fractions

1. Find the related common denominator each fraction and then add the fraction

a. $\frac{1}{2} + \frac{1}{3} =$

b. $\frac{1}{5} + \frac{1}{2} =$

c. $\frac{1}{3} + \frac{2}{5} =$

d. $\frac{1}{4} + \frac{1}{3} =$

2. Add these fractions. Change the improper fractions to a mixed numeral.

a. $\frac{1}{2} + \frac{3}{4} =$ _____

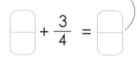

b. $\frac{4}{5} + \frac{2}{3} =$ _____

c. $\frac{3}{5} + \frac{3}{4} =$ _____

d. $\frac{2}{3} + \frac{1}{2} =$ _____

3. Find the related common denominator each fraction and then find the differen

a. $\frac{4}{5} - \frac{1}{2} =$

b. $\frac{3}{4} - \frac{1}{3} =$

c. $\frac{7}{8} - \frac{1}{2} =$

d. $\frac{2}{3} - \frac{1}{4} =$

e. $\frac{3}{4} - \frac{1}{5} =$

f. $\frac{1}{2} - \frac{1}{3} =$

Area

Find the area of each 2D shape. (Not to scale).

a.
4cm
cm | Area = ____ cm²

b.
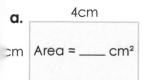
2cm
Area = ____ cm²
6cm

c.
4cm
cm | Area = ____ cm²
5cm

d.
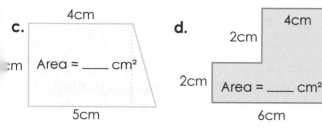
4cm
2cm
2cm | Area = ____ cm²
6cm

Using the formula L X B, calculate the area of the rectangles in this table.

Rectangle	a	b	c	d
Length (L)	4cm	8cm	7cm	9cm
Breadth (B)	3cm	4cm	5cm	3cm
Area				

Find the lengths of the other side/s in each rectangle. (Not to scale).

a.
5cm
Area = 15cm²
____ cm

b.
6cm
Area = 24cm²
____ cm

c.
8cm
Area = 32cm²
____ cm

Find the area of these home or school items.

a.

Height = ____ cm
Length = ____ cm
Area = ____ cm

b.

Height = ____ cm
Length = ____ cm
Area = ____ cm

c.

Height = ____ cm   Length = ____ cm
Area = ____ cm

Graphs and Data

A car travelled for 8 hours at an average speed of 70 kilometres per hour. The car stopped for half an hour every 2 hours.

1. Plot the journey and join the points to make a line graph.

Time	1hr	2hr	3hr	4hr	5hr	6hr	7hr	8hr
Distance	70	140	175	245	315	350	420	490

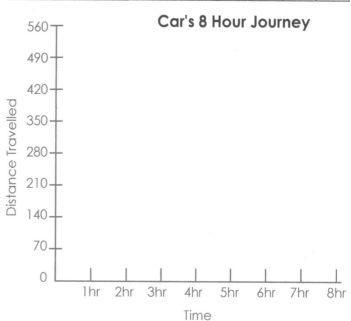

Car's 8 Hour Journey

2. a. At what distance was the first rest break taken? _____

b. How far had the car travelled after 3 ½ hours? _____

c. How long had the car been on the road when it stopped a second time? _____

d. How far had the car travelled in 6 hours? _____

e. How long did it take to travel 420 km? _____

f. How far did the car travel in its last 3 hours? _____

3. After a half hour break at the 8 hour point, how far would the car travel in 9 hours? _____

4. Continuing at the same speed, what distance would be travelled in 10 hours? _____

55

Pascal's Triangle

PASCAL'S TRIANGLE

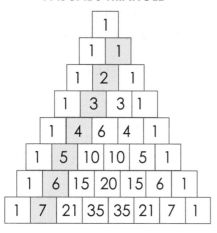

TOTALS

a.
b.
c.
d.
e.
f.
g.
h.

1. Write the sum of each line of the triangle.

2. Write the triangular numbers showing on Pascal's Triangle.

3. Add the two triangular numbers that give each square number. (Look at Pascal's triangle).

a. ☐ + ☐ = 4   b. ☐ + ☐ = 36

c. ☐ + ☐ = 9   d. ☐ + ☐ = 25

e. ☐ + ☐ = 16   f. ☐ + ☐ = 49

4. Fill in the numbers from the lines in the triangle that have symmetry.

a.

b.

c.

5. Write the square of each number.

a. 2^2 = ☐   b. 4^2 = ☐   c. 6^2 = ☐

d. 5^2 = ☐   e. 3^2 = ☐   f. 7^2 = ☐

Division

1. Complete each number sentence. Do the brackets first.

a. $(7 + 5) \div 4 =$ ☐   b. $(8 + 2) \div 5 =$ ☐

c. $(42 \div 6) + 7 =$ ☐   d. $(7 + 2) \div 3 =$ ☐

e. $(37 - 16) \div 7 =$ ☐   f. $(12 \div 2) + 2 =$ ☐

g. $(12 + 4) \div 2 =$ ☐   h. $(36 \times \frac{1}{2}) \div 6 =$ ☐

2. Complete each division algorithm. Write the remainder as a fraction.

a. $2\overline{)5135}$ r   b. $4\overline{)6143}$ r   c. $5\overline{)4362}$ r

d. $10\overline{)7137}$ r   e. $4\overline{)5165}$ r   f. $5\overline{)6273}$ r

3. Write the remainder to each division to two decimal places.

a. $4\overline{)5317.0}$ r   b. $3\overline{)4528.0}$ r

c. $5\overline{)3821.0}$ r   d. $2\overline{)6417.0}$ r

e. $7\overline{)8352.0}$ r   f. $6\overline{)2759.0}$ r

4. Match the division algorithm to the number closest to its answer.

a. $24\overline{)2374}$ 155   b. $46\overline{)712}$

147

c. $43\overline{)6320}$ 99   d. $72\overline{)930}$

129

Length and Distance

Time and Timetables

Use the scaled map to find distances in kilometres. (Scale 10 mm = 2 km)

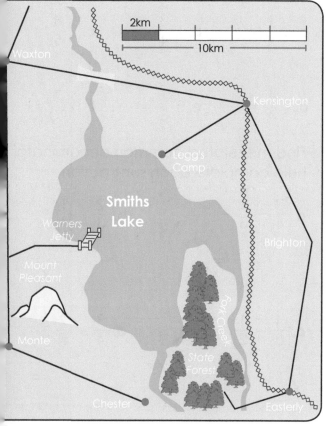

How far from Waxton is the bridge across the stream that flows into Smiths Lake. ☐ km

A car broke down 3 cm from Chester on the way to Monte. How far is this in kilometres? ☐ km

Shaylene lives 2 km from Legg's Camp. What is this in mm on the map? ☐

Use a piece of string to find the perimeter of Smiths Lake. ☐ km

How many kilometres are represented by 85 mm on this map? ☐ km

A real distance of 10 km is what length on the map? ☐ mm

Mark tows his boat from Chester to Warners Jetty each weekend. How far is the round trip? ☐ km

Write each distance in decimal notation.

a. 2 kilometres 850 metres _____

b. 7200m _____

c. $\frac{1}{4}$ kilometres _____

d. 420m _____

e. 800 metres _____

f. $1\frac{3}{4}$ km _____

1. Write the adjusted time for each situation.

a. A train is to arrive at 7:54 am. It is 43 minutes late. What time will it arrive? _____

b. The bus left the midnight run 11 minutes early. Write its departure time in 24-hour time.

c. Dad was late for work by 47 minutes. If he is on afternoon shift and arrived at 13:07 what was his usual starting time? _____

d. A car travelled at 80 kilometres per hour for 2 ¼ hours. How far did the car travel in that time? _____

2. Write each digital, 24-hour time as am or pm time.

a. 13:27 **b.** 15:55 **c.** 18:02

_____ _____ _____

d. 17:35 **e.** 23:56 **f.** 16:19

_____ _____ _____

3. Write the analogue times in 24-hour, afternoon time.

 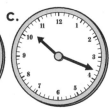

a. **b.** **c.**

_____ _____ _____

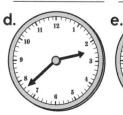  

d. **e.** **f.**

_____ _____ _____

4. A bus arrived 15 minutes late. If it was scheduled to arrive at 11:55 what time did it arrive? _____

57

Place Value

1. Write the eight-digit number represented on each abacus.

a.

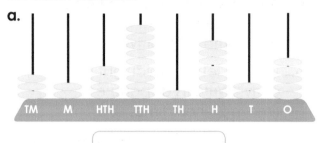

b.

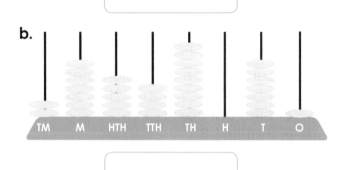

2. What is the place value of one in question a?

3. Arrange 2,8,7,6,1,4,3,0 to make the **largest** possible number.

4. Round off 93 817 600 to the **nearest** ten million.

5. Identify the place value as thousandths, hundredths, tenths, ones, hundreds or thousands for each circled numeral.

a. 6 7 3 . 4 8 5   **b.** 6 2 . 8 3 6

_____   _____

c. 4 3 5 . 5 1 9   **d.** 6 5 8 . 7 5 2

_____   _____

6. Subtract the number and then write the new 8-digit number.

a. 62 358 724 less 25 600   _____

b. 82 493 7678 less 587 200   _____

c. 12 432 516 less 186 900   _____

58 d. 41 637 285 less 154 200   _____

Fractions

1. Change each mixed numeral into an improper fraction.

a. $3\frac{1}{2} =$ ⬭   **b.** $1\frac{3}{4} =$ ⬭   **c.** $2\frac{4}{5} =$ ⬭

d. $4\frac{1}{4} =$ ⬭   **e.** $3\frac{1}{3} =$ ⬭   **f.** $1\frac{7}{10} =$ ⬭

2. Find the related common denominator help complete each subtraction.

a. $\frac{3}{4} - \frac{1}{3} =$ ____

⬭ − ⬭ = ⬭

b. $\frac{2}{3} - \frac{1}{4} =$ ____

⬭ − ⬭ = ⬭

c. $\frac{4}{5} - \frac{1}{2} =$ ____

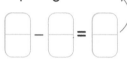

d. $\frac{3}{4} - \frac{2}{5} =$ ____

⬭ + ⬭ = ⬭

e. $\frac{9}{10} - \frac{3}{5} =$ ____

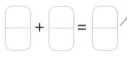

$\frac{9}{10} -$ ⬭ = ⬭

f. $\frac{7}{8} - \frac{3}{4} =$ ____

$\frac{7}{8} -$ ⬭ = ⬭

3. Change each mixed numeral into an improper fraction and then subtract. Change improper fractions to mixed numerals in the answers.

a. $\frac{4}{5} - \frac{1}{2} =$

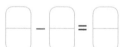

b. $\frac{3}{4} - \frac{1}{3} =$

⬭ + ⬭ = ⬭

c. $\frac{7}{8} - \frac{1}{2} =$

d. $\frac{2}{3} - \frac{1}{4} =$

⬭ − ⬭ = ⬭

4. Change each improper fraction into a mixed numeral.

a. $\frac{9}{6} =$ ____ **b.** $\frac{7}{4} =$ ____ **c.** $\frac{8}{5} =$ ____ **d.** $\frac{6}{2} =$ __

Prisms/Pyramids

Count the faces, vertices and edges on each 3D object.

a.
☐ faces
☐ vertices
☐ edges

b.
☐ faces
☐ vertices
☐ edges

c.
☐ faces
☐ vertices
☐ edges

d.
☐ faces
☐ vertices
☐ edges

e.
☐ faces
☐ vertices
☐ edges

f.
☐ faces
☐ vertices
☐ edges

g.
☐ faces
☐ vertices
☐ edges

h.
☐ faces
☐ vertices
☐ edges

i.
☐ faces
☐ vertices
☐ edges

Label the views showing for each object.

a.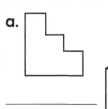
_____ _____

_____

b.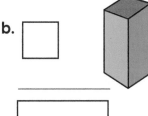
_____

_____

What 3D solid can be made from each net?

a.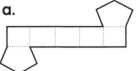
_____

b.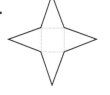
_____

Chance

1. Write, as a percentage, the chance of landing on number 7 on each spinner.

a.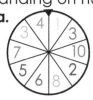
b.
c.

_____%   _____%   _____%

d.
e.
f.

_____%   _____%   _____%

2. Write, as a fraction, the change of each event happening.

a. Roll an odd number on a die. _____

b. Roll a 4 on a die. _____

c. Choose a diamond card from a standard pack of cards. _____

d. Toss two heads with 3 coins. _____

e. Roll an eight with a standard die. _____

3. PROBLEMS

a. A boy has 5 oranges, 3 apples and 2 bananas. Write, as a percentage, the chance of selecting a banana.

_____%

b. Write, as a fraction, the chance of choosing an apple if there are 6 apples, 2 bananas and 2 oranges. ☐

4. Toss a coin ten times and record the results.

a. What percentage of heads turned up? _____%

b. What fraction of tails turned up? ☐

c. If the coin toss was repeated would the results be the same? Tick your choice.

Yes ☐   No ☐

59

Answers

Unit 1	**Place Value: 1a.**1 379 524 **b.** 7 350 426 **2a.** 3 ten thousand **b.** 5 hundreds **c.** 4 hundred thousand **d.** 8 ones **e.** 3 million **3a.** 6 254 004 **b.** 7 443 817 **c.**8 135 176 **d.** 3 300 652 **4a.** 6 million **b.** 66 milli **c.** 4 million **d.** 2 million **5a.** 7 239 866 **b.** 2 466 024 **c.** 3 320 145 **d.** 4 173 650 **Addition: 1a.** 5 806 410 **b.** 407 568 **c.** 8 007 956 **2a.** 126 543 **b.** 171 683 **3a.** 90 916 **b.** 85 951 **c.** 100 888 **4.** 174 027 **5.a.** $1018.45 **b.** $1133.23 **c.** $881.68 **6.** 91726 **Length: 1a.** 22mm **b.** 32mm **c.** 38mm **d.** 42mm **e.** 10cm **f.** 7m **2a.** 30m **b.** 45m **c.** 60m **d.** 40m **e.** 50m **2a.** 10mm **b.** 1 metre **c.** 1000 metres **d.** 4cm **e.** 4000m **f.** 1/2km **3.** answers will vary, approx **a.** 150mm **b.** 50mm **c.** 160mm **d.** 150mm **e.** 210mm **f.** 25mm **Time: 1.** Parent/Teacher **2a.**1811 **b.**1950 **c.** 1913 **d.** 2025 **e.** 2105 **f.** 1555 **3a.** 1952 **b.** 0037 **c.** 1236 **d.** 11 **4a.** 0730 **b.** 0450 **c.** 2320 **d.** 1945 **e.** 0013 **f.** 2052 **5a.** 11:45pm **b.** 11:50am **c.** 12:30am **d.** 12:30pm
Unit 2	**Prime and Composite Numbers: 1.** 2,3,5,7,11,13,17,19,23,29,31 **2a.** 1,2,4,8 **b.** 1,2,4,8,16 **c.** 1,2,3,4,6,8,12,24 **d.** 1,2,4,7,14,28 **3.** 8 **4.** 77 **5.** 3 and 5 **6a.** 2x6→2x2x3 **b.** 2x8→2x2x2x2 **c.** 5x2x2 **7a.** 60 **b.** 210 **c.** 90 **Subtraction: 1a.** 3 215 **b.** 3 214 **c.** 2 233 **2a.** 52 079 **b.** 13 088 **c.** 55 779 **d.** 25 179 **3a.** 2 269/4 41 64 343 **b.** 542/2 683/ 62 616 **c.** 1 229/3 370/ 63 303 **d.** 2 418/ 4 559/ 64 492 **4a.** $163.11 **b.** $330.85 **c.** $139.71 **5.** 4 877 sheep **Length: 1a.** 14cm **b.** 10cm **c.** 12cm **d.** 18cm **e.** 20cm **2a.** 4.53km **b.** 2.75km **c.** 10.24km **d.** 0.45km **e.** 0.027km **3a.** 3.8m **b.** 7.25km **c.** 2.5m **d.** 0.628km **e.** 0.75m **4a.** 56mm **b.** 48mm **c.** 43mm **Transformation: 1a.** ⬆ **b.** ⬇ **c.** ◣ **d.** ➡ **2a.** flip **b.**turn **c.** slide **3** b,c,d,e **4.** /\/\/\/\
Unit 3	**Rounding Off: 1a.** 660 **b.** 840 **c.** 380 **d.** 640 **e.** 720 **f.** 550 **2a.** 700 **b.** 800 **c.** 400 **d.** 600 **e.** 700 **f.** 5(**3a.** 5 000 **b.** 6 000 **c.** 8000 **d.** 6000 **e.** 8000 **f.** 5000 **4.** 3304→3000, 2750→3000, 5380 →5000, 68 →7000, 7100 →7000, 4437→4000 **5a.** ≈ 900 **b.** ≈ 600 **c.** ≈ 900 **d.** ≈ 700 **6a.** ≈ 16 000 **b.** ≈ 8 000 **Mulitplication: 1a.** 3 702 **b.** $455.07 **c.** 12 698 **c.** 19 025 **d.** 98 728 **e.** 198 762 **f.** 49 611 **2.** 978/ 3 735/ 11 436/ 2 571/ 10 089/ 12 843/ 2 301 **3a.** 1 408 **b.** 2 256 **c.** 9 500 **d.** 8 825 **4a.** $79.89 **b.** $244.65 **c.** $350.08 **d.** 470.22 **e.** 4 550.70 **Mass: 1a.** 85g **b.** 385kg **c.** 600g **d.** 48kg **e.** 2T **f.** 2g **2a.** 41kg **b.** 31kg **c.** 89kg **3a.** 4kg **b.** 1/2kg **c.** 3/4kg **d.** 9.5kg **4a.** 10 **b.** 15 **c.** 500g **5.** 4kg **6.** 7kg **Graphs: 1.** 3 hours **2.** 120km **3.** 2 **4.** 1 hr **5.** 60km **6.** 60km **7.** 8hrs **8.** 6 1/2hrs **9.** 2 hrs **10.** 1 1/2 hrs **10.** 1 1/2 hrs **12.** 10 hrs without a break.
Unit 4	**Square Numbers: 1a.** 4 **b.** 9 **c.** 16 **d.** 25 **e.** 49 **f.** 36 **2.** 36/100/25/64/121/81 **3a.** 29 **b.** 71 **c.** 29 **d.** 65 **e.** 90 **f.** 19 **g.** 20 **h.** 65 **i.** 53 **4.** 121,144,169,196 **5a.** 9 **b.** 11 **c.** 13 **d.** 15 **6.** 13,15,17 **7a.** $3^2+7=16=4^2$ **b.** $4^2+9=25=5^2$ **Division: 1a.** 57r1 **b.** 151r1 **c.** 35r1 **d.** 64r1 **e.** 68r1 **f.** 75r2 **g.** 154r1 **h.** 267r1 **i.** 146r2 **2a.** 169r2 5)847 **b.** 77r1 5)386 **c.** 122r0 6)732 **d.** 214r0 4)856 **3a.** 1 341 **b.** 576r1 **c.** 841r1 **d.** 1341r4 **e.** 153r1 **f.** 1650r1 **4a.** $30/h **b.** 40km **Mass/Volume: 1a.** 24cm³ **b.** 30cm³ **c.** 50cm³ **2a.** 75mL **b.** 50mL **c.** 20mL **d.** 16mL **3a.** 200g **b.** 50(**4a.** 8L **b.** 200mL **c.** 375mL **5a.** 600g **b.** 350cm³ **c.** 750g **d.** 500cm³ **e.** 250g **f.** 1.2kg **Location: 1.** B3 **2.** D6 **3.** E3 **4.** B7 **5.** C4 **6.** D1 **7.** F7 **8.** A5 **9.** F1 **10.** A1 **2.** 90° East, 135 SE, 180° south, 225° SW, 270° west, 315° NW **3.** Teacher/parent
Unit 5	**Triangular Numbers: 1a.** 3 **b.**6 **c.** 10 **d.** 15 **e.** 21 **f.** 28 **2a.** 28 **b.** 55 **c.** 36 **d.** 21 **3a.** 11 **b.** 9 **c.** 13 **d.** 6 **e.** 15 **f.** 7 **4a.** 16 **b.** 28+36=64 **c.** 49 **d.** 100 **e.** 36+45=81 **5.** 3,6,10,15,21,28,36,45 **Equivalent Fractions: 1a.** 12% **b.** 37% **c.** 52% **d.** 30% **e.** 4% **f.**27% **2a.** [grid] **b.** [grid] **c.** [grid] **d.** [grid] **e.** [grid] **f.** [grid] **3a.** 1/10 **b.** 7/10 **c.** 5/10 | 1/2 **d.** 2/10 | 1/5 **e.** 6/10 |3/5 **f.** 9/10 **g.** 3/10 **h.** 1/4 **i.** 3/4 **j.** 8/10 | 4/5 **4a.** 0.2 **b.** 0.4 **c.** 7/10 **d.** 20% **e.** 1/3 **f.** 0.4 **5a.** 0.5 **b.** 0.75 **Prisms and Pyramids: 1a.** triangular prism **b.** rectangular prism **c.** hexagonal pyramid **d.** square pyramid **e.** octagonal prism **f.** cone **2a.** 7 faces 10 corners **b.** 6 faces 8 corners **c.** 5 faces 5 corners **d.** 5 faces 6 corners **3a.** cylinder **b.** square pyramid **c.** hexagonal pyramid **d.** cube **Timetable: 1.** hourly **2.** 1 hour 11 minutes **3.** 1 hour 31 minutes **4.** 1319 **5.** 1419 **6.** 14 minutes **7.** 1203 **8.** 15:41 **9.** 12:35
Unit 6	**Integers: 1a.** 7 **b.** 5 **c.** 7 **d.** 70 **2a.** +1 **b.** -4 **c.** -4 **d.** -5 **e.** -5 **f.** -3 **g.** +4 **h.** -6 **3a.** 4°C **b.** -9°C **c.** -7°C **d.** 7°C **e.** -1°C **4a.** [number line] **b.** [number line] **c.** [number line] **d.** [number line] **e.** [number line] **5a.** -5 **b.** -15 **c.** -6 **Fractions: 1a.** 2/5 **b.** 3/4 **c.** 3/5 **d.** 1/2 **e.** 1/2 **f.** 1/4 **g.** 1/3 **h.** 1/4 **i.** 3/5 **2a.** 2/4 + 1/4 = 3/4 **b.** 4/10 + 1/10 = 5/10 = 1/2 **c.** 5/8 + 2/8 = 7/8 **d.** 4/6 + 1/6 = 5/6 **e.** 6/8 + 1/8 = 7/8 **f.** 3/10 + 4/10 = 7/10 **3a.** 7/8 - 2/8 = 5/8 **b.** 7/10 - 4/10 = 3/10 **c.** 2/4 - 1/4 = 1/4 **d.** 5/8 - 4/8 = 1/8 **e.** 3/4 - 2/4 = 1/4 **f.** 9/10 - 5/10 = 4/10 / 2/5 **4a.** 10 **b.** 4 **c.** 2 **Area: 1a.** 24cm² **b.** 36cm² **c.** 9cm² **d.** 60cm² **2a.** 2cm **b.** 6cm **c.** 4cm **3a.** 21cm² **b.** 17cm² **4a.** 24cm² **b.** 3cm **c.** 12cm²

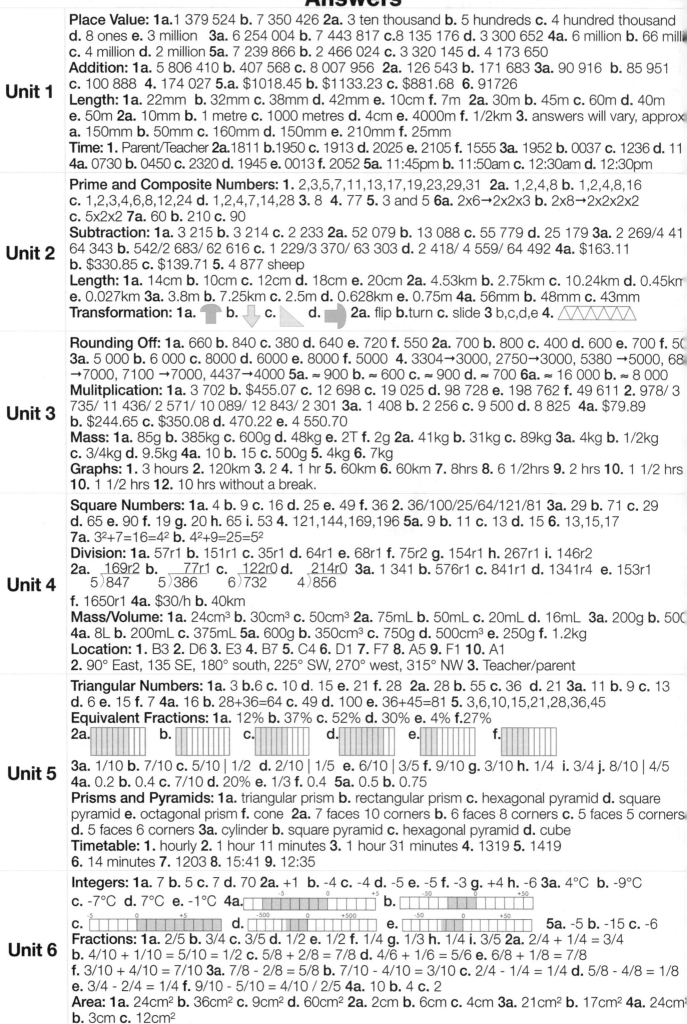

60

Answers

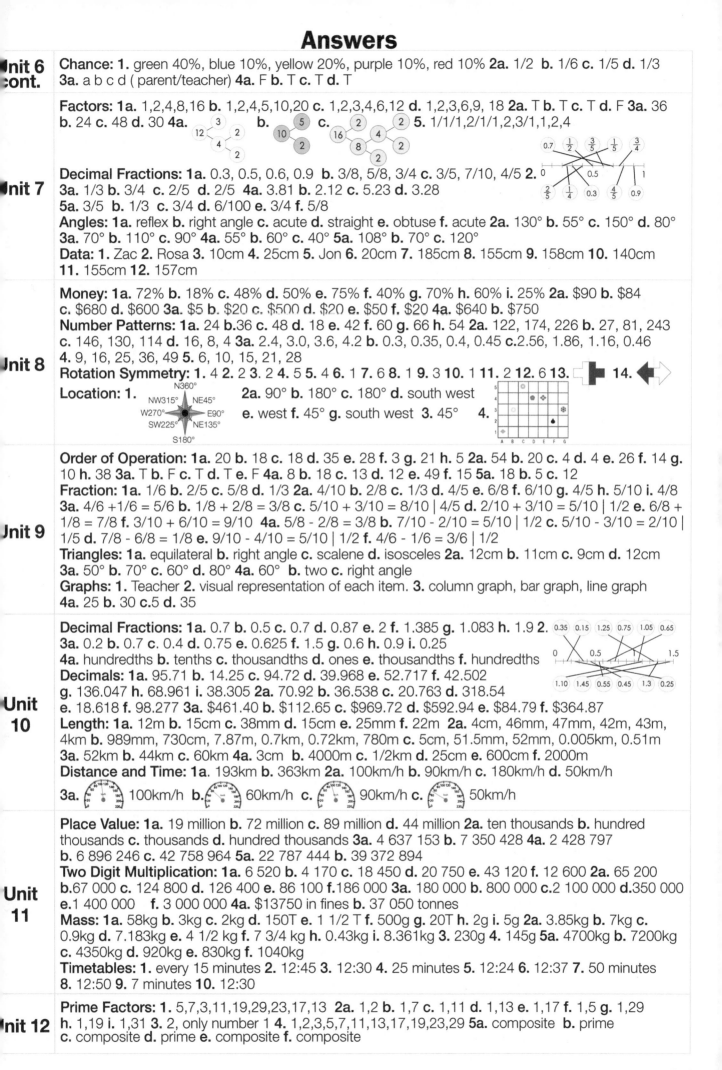

Unit 6 cont. Chance: **1.** green 40%, blue 10%, yellow 20%, purple 10%, red 10% **2a.** 1/2 **b.** 1/6 **c.** 1/5 **d.** 1/3 **3a.** a b c d (parent/teacher) **4a.** F **b.** T **c.** T **d.** T

Unit 7 Factors: **1a.** 1,2,4,8,16 **b.** 1,2,4,5,10,20 **c.** 1,2,3,4,6,12 **d.** 1,2,3,6,9, 18 **2a.** T **b.** T **c.** T **d.** F **3a.** 36 **b.** 24 **c.** 48 **d.** 30 **4a.** [diagram] **b.** [diagram] **c.** [diagram] **5.** 1/1/1,2/1/1,2,3/1,1,2,4

Decimal Fractions: **1a.** 0.3, 0.5, 0.6, 0.9 **b.** 3/8, 5/8, 3/4 **c.** 3/5, 7/10, 4/5 **2.** [number line]
3a. 1/3 **b.** 3/4 **c.** 2/5 **d.** 2/5 **4a.** 3.81 **b.** 2.12 **c.** 5.23 **d.** 3.28
5a. 3/5 **b.** 1/3 **c.** 3/4 **d.** 6/100 **e.** 3/4 **f.** 5/8

Angles: **1a.** reflex **b.** right angle **c.** acute **d.** straight **e.** obtuse **f.** acute **2a.** 130° **b.** 55° **c.** 150° **d.** 80°
3a. 70° **b.** 110° **c.** 90° **4a.** 55° **b.** 60° **c.** 40° **5a.** 108° **b.** 70° **c.** 120°

Data: **1.** Zac **2.** Rosa **3.** 10cm **4.** 25cm **5.** Jon **6.** 20cm **7.** 185cm **8.** 155cm **9.** 158cm **10.** 140cm
11. 155cm **12.** 157cm

Unit 8 Money: **1a.** 72% **b.** 18% **c.** 48% **d.** 50% **e.** 75% **f.** 40% **g.** 70% **h.** 60% **i.** 25% **2a.** $90 **b.** $84
c. $680 **d.** $600 **3a.** $5 **b.** $20 **c.** $500 **d.** $20 **e.** $50 **f.** $20 **4a.** $640 **b.** $750

Number Patterns: **1a.** 24 **b.**36 **c.** 48 **d.** 18 **e.** 42 **f.** 60 **g.** 66 **h.** 54 **2a.** 122, 174, 226 **b.** 27, 81, 243
c. 146, 130, 114 **d.** 16, 8, 4 **3a.** 2.4, 3.0, 3.6, 4.2 **b.** 0.3, 0.35, 0.4, 0.45 **c.**2.56, 1.86, 1.16, 0.46
4. 9, 16, 25, 36, 49 **5.** 6, 10, 15, 21, 28

Rotation Symmetry: **1.** 4 **2.** 2 **3.** 2 **4.** 5 **5.** 4 **6.** 1 **7.** 6 **8.** 1 **9.** 3 **10.** 1 **11.** 2 **12.** 6 **13.** [shape] **14.** [arrow]

Location: **1.** [compass diagram N360° NW315° NE45° W270° E90° SW225° NE135° S180°] **2a.** 90° **b.** 180° **c.** 180° **d.** south west
e. west **f.** 45° **g.** south west **3.** 45° **4.** [grid diagram]

Unit 9 Order of Operation: **1a.** 20 **b.** 18 **c.** 18 **d.** 35 **e.** 28 **f.** 3 **g.** 21 **h.** 5 **2a.** 54 **b.** 20 **c.** 4 **d.** 4 **e.** 26 **f.** 14 **g.**
10 **h.** 38 **3a.** T **b.** F **c.** T **d.** T **e.** F **4a.** 8 **b.** 18 **c.** 13 **d.** 12 **e.** 49 **f.** 15 **5a.** 18 **b.** 5 **c.** 12

Fraction: **1a.** 1/6 **b.** 2/5 **c.** 5/8 **d.** 1/3 **2a.** 4/10 **b.** 2/8 **c.** 1/3 **d.** 4/5 **e.** 6/8 **f.** 6/10 **g.** 4/5 **h.** 5/10 **i.** 4/8
3a. 4/6 +1/6 = 5/6 **b.** 1/8 + 2/8 = 3/8 **c.** 5/10 + 3/10 = 8/10 | 4/5 **d.** 2/10 + 3/10 = 5/10 | 1/2 **e.** 6/8 +
1/8 = 7/8 **f.** 3/10 + 6/10 = 9/10 **4a.** 5/8 - 2/8 = 3/8 **b.** 7/10 - 2/10 = 5/10 | 1/2 **c.** 5/10 - 3/10 = 2/10 |
1/5 **d.** 7/8 - 6/8 = 1/8 **e.** 9/10 - 4/10 = 5/10 | 1/2 **f.** 4/6 - 1/6 = 3/6 | 1/2

Triangles: **1a.** equilateral **b.** right angle **c.** scalene **d.** isosceles **2a.** 12cm **b.** 11cm **c.** 9cm **d.** 12cm
3a. 50° **b.** 70° **c.** 60° **d.** 80° **4a.** 60° **b.** two **c.** right angle

Graphs: **1.** Teacher **2.** visual representation of each item. **3.** column graph, bar graph, line graph
4a. 25 **b.** 30 **c.**5 **d.** 35

Unit 10 Decimal Fractions: **1a.** 0.7 **b.** 0.5 **c.** 0.7 **d.** 0.87 **e.** 2 **f.** 1.385 **g.** 1.083 **h.** 1.9 **2.** [number line]
3a. 0.2 **b.** 0.7 **c.** 0.4 **d.** 0.75 **e.** 0.625 **f.** 1.5 **g.** 0.6 **h.** 0.9 **i.** 0.25
4a. hundredths **b.** tenths **c.** thousandths **d.** ones **e.** thousandths **f.** hundredths

Decimals: **1a.** 95.71 **b.** 14.25 **c.** 94.72 **d.** 39.968 **e.** 52.717 **f.** 42.502
g. 136.047 **h.** 68.961 **i.** 38.305 **2a.** 70.92 **b.** 36.538 **c.** 20.763 **d.** 318.54
e. 18.618 **f.** 98.277 **3a.** $461.40 **b.** $112.65 **c.** $969.72 **d.** $592.94 **e.** $84.79 **f.** $364.87

Length: **1a.** 12m **b.** 15cm **c.** 38mm **d.** 15cm **e.** 25mm **f.** 22m **2a.** 4cm, 46mm, 47mm, 42m, 43m,
4km **b.** 989mm, 730cm, 7.87m, 0.7km, 0.72km, 780m **c.** 5cm, 51.5mm, 52mm, 0.005km, 0.51m
3a. 52km **b.** 44km **c.** 60km **4a.** 3cm **b.** 4000m **c.** 1/2km **d.** 25cm **e.** 600cm **f.** 2000m

Distance and Time: **1a.** 193km **b.** 363km **2a.** 100km/h **b.** 90km/h **c.** 180km/h **d.** 50km/h

3a. [gauge] 100km/h **b.** [gauge] 60km/h **c.** [gauge] 90km/h **c.** [gauge] 50km/h

Unit 11 Place Value: **1a.** 19 million **b.** 72 million **c.** 89 million **d.** 44 million **2a.** ten thousands **b.** hundred
thousands **c.** thousands **d.** hundred thousands **3a.** 4 637 153 **b.** 7 350 428 **4a.** 2 428 797
b. 6 896 246 **c.** 42 758 964 **5a.** 22 787 444 **b.** 39 372 894

Two Digit Multiplication: **1a.** 6 520 **b.** 4 170 **c.** 18 450 **d.** 20 750 **e.** 43 120 **f.** 12 600 **2a.** 65 200
b.67 000 **c.** 124 800 **d.** 126 400 **e.** 86 100 **f.**186 000 **3a.** 180 000 **b.** 800 000 **c.**2 100 000 **d.**350 000
e.1 400 000 **f.** 3 000 000 **4a.** $13750 in fines **b.** 37 050 tonnes

Mass: **1a.** 58kg **b.** 3kg **c.** 2kg **d.** 150T **e.** 1 1/2 T **f.** 500g **g.** 20T **h.** 2g **i.** 5g **2a.** 3.85kg **b.** 7kg **c.**
0.9kg **d.** 7.183kg **e.** 4 1/2 kg **f.** 7 3/4 kg **h.** 0.43kg **i.** 8.361kg **3.** 230g **4.** 145g **5a.** 4700kg **b.** 7200kg
c. 4350kg **d.** 920kg **e.** 830kg **f.** 1040kg

Timetables: **1.** every 15 minutes **2.** 12:45 **3.** 12:30 **4.** 25 minutes **5.** 12:24 **6.** 12:37 **7.** 50 minutes
8. 12:50 **9.** 7 minutes **10.** 12:30

Unit 12 Prime Factors: **1.** 5,7,3,11,19,29,23,17,13 **2a.** 1,2 **b.** 1,7 **c.** 1,11 **d.** 1,13 **e.** 1,17 **f.** 1,5 **g.** 1,29
h. 1,19 **i.** 1,31 **3.** 2, only number 1 **4.** 1,2,3,5,7,11,13,17,19,23,29 **5a.** composite **b.** prime
c. composite **d.** prime **e.** composite **f.** composite

Answers

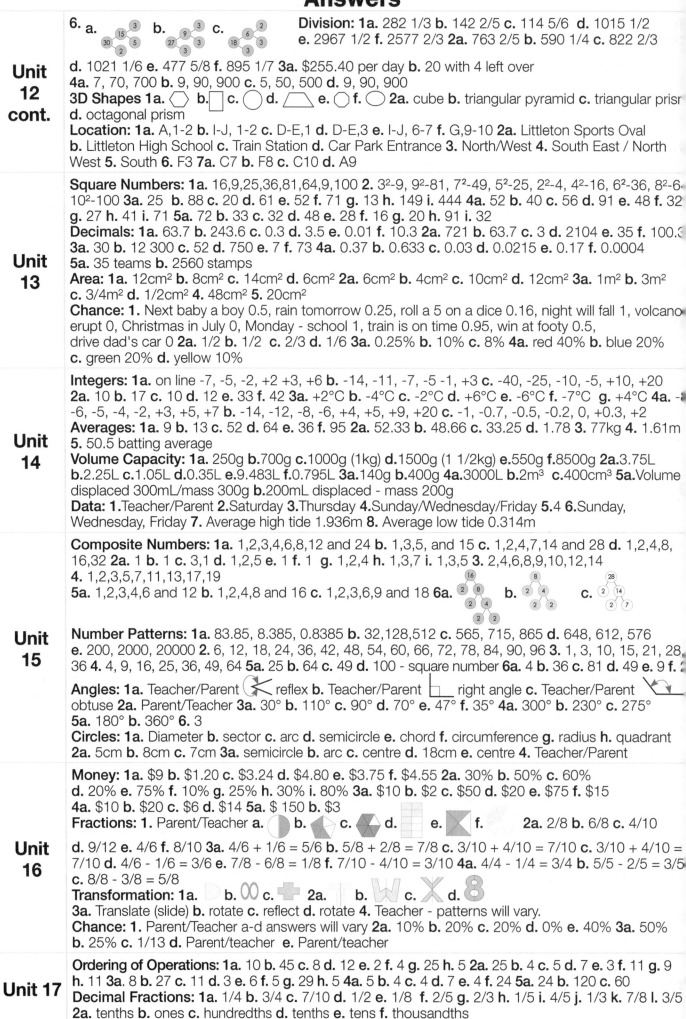

Unit 12 cont.

6. a. **b.** **c.** **Division: 1a.** 282 1/3 **b.** 142 2/5 **c.** 114 5/6 **d.** 1015 1/2 **e.** 2967 1/2 **f.** 2577 2/3 **2a.** 763 2/5 **b.** 590 1/4 **c.** 822 2/3 **d.** 1021 1/6 **e.** 477 5/8 **f.** 895 1/7 **3a.** $255.40 per day **b.** 20 with 4 left over **4a.** 7, 70, 700 **b.** 9, 90, 900 **c.** 5, 50, 500 **d.** 9, 90, 900

3D Shapes 1a. ⬡ **b.** ☐ **c.** ◯ **d.** ▱ **e.** ◯ **f.** ◯ **2a.** cube **b.** triangular pyramid **c.** triangular prism **d.** octagonal prism

Location: 1a. A,1-2 **b.** I-J, 1-2 **c.** D-E,1 **d.** D-E,3 **e.** I-J, 6-7 **f.** G,9-10 **2a.** Littleton Sports Oval **b.** Littleton High School **c.** Train Station **d.** Car Park Entrance **3.** North/West **4.** South East / North West **5.** South **6.** F3 **7a.** C7 **b.** F8 **c.** C10 **d.** A9

Unit 13

Square Numbers: 1a. 16,9,25,36,81,64,9,100 **2.** 3²-9, 9²-81, 7²-49, 5²-25, 2²-4, 4²-16, 6²-36, 8²-64, 10²-100 **3a.** 25 **b.** 88 **c.** 20 **d.** 61 **e.** 52 **f.** 71 **g.** 13 **h.** 149 **i.** 444 **4a.** 52 **b.** 40 **c.** 56 **d.** 91 **e.** 48 **f.** 32 **g.** 27 **h.** 41 **i.** 71 **5a.** 72 **b.** 33 **c.** 32 **d.** 48 **e.** 28 **f.** 16 **g.** 20 **h.** 91 **i.** 32

Decimals: 1a. 63.7 **b.** 243.6 **c.** 0.3 **d.** 3.5 **e.** 0.01 **f.** 10.3 **2a.** 721 **b.** 63.7 **c.** 3 **d.** 2104 **e.** 35 **f.** 100.3 **3a.** 30 **b.** 12 300 **c.** 52 **d.** 750 **e.** 7 **f.** 73 **4a.** 0.37 **b.** 0.633 **c.** 0.03 **d.** 0.0215 **e.** 0.17 **f.** 0.0004 **5a.** 35 teams **b.** 2560 stamps

Area: 1a. 12cm² **b.** 8cm² **c.** 14cm² **d.** 6cm² **2a.** 6cm² **b.** 4cm² **c.** 10cm² **d.** 12cm² **3a.** 1m² **b.** 3m² **c.** 3/4m² **d.** 1/2cm² **4.** 48cm² **5.** 20cm²

Chance: 1. Next baby a boy 0.5, rain tomorrow 0.25, roll a 5 on a dice 0.16, night will fall 1, volcano erupt 0, Christmas in July 0, Monday - school 1, train is on time 0.95, win at footy 0.5, drive dad's car 0 **2a.** 1/2 **b.** 1/2 **c.** 2/3 **d.** 1/6 **3a.** 0.25% **b.** 10% **c.** 8% **4a.** red 40% **b.** blue 20% **c.** green 20% **d.** yellow 10%

Unit 14

Integers: 1a. on line -7, -5, -2, +2 +3, +6 **b.** -14, -11, -7, -5 -1, +3 **c.** -40, -25, -10, -5, +10, +20 **2a.** 10 **b.** 17 **c.** 10 **d.** 12 **e.** 33 **f.** 42 **3a.** +2°C **b.** -4°C **c.** -2°C **d.** +6°C **e.** -6°C **f.** -7°C **g.** +4°C **4a.** -6, -5, -4, -2, +3, +5, +7 **b.** -14, -12, -8, -6, +4, +5, +9, +20 **c.** -1, -0.7, -0.5, -0.2, 0, +0.3, +2

Averages: 1a. 9 **b.** 13 **c.** 52 **d.** 64 **e.** 36 **f.** 95 **2a.** 52.33 **b.** 48.66 **c.** 33.25 **d.** 1.78 **3.** 77kg **4.** 1.61m **5.** 50.5 batting average

Volume Capacity: 1a. 250g **b.** 700g **c.** 1000g (1kg) **d.** 1500g (1 1/2kg) **e.** 550g **f.** 8500g **2a.** 3.75L **b.** 2.25L **c.** 1.05L **d.** 0.35L **e.** 9.483L **f.** 0.795L **3a.** 140g **b.** 400g **4a.** 3000L **b.** 2m³ **c.** 400cm³ **5a.** Volume displaced 300mL/mass 300g **b.** 200mL displaced - mass 200g

Data: 1. Teacher/Parent **2.** Saturday **3.** Thursday **4.** Sunday/Wednesday/Friday **5.** 4 **6.** Sunday, Wednesday, Friday **7.** Average high tide 1.936m **8.** Average low tide 0.314m

Unit 15

Composite Numbers: 1a. 1,2,3,4,6,8,12 and 24 **b.** 1,3,5, and 15 **c.** 1,2,4,7,14 and 28 **d.** 1,2,4,8, 16,32 **2a.** 1 **b.** 1 **c.** 3,1 **d.** 1,2,5 **e.** 1 **f.** 1 **g.** 1,2,4 **h.** 1,3,7 **i.** 1,3,5 **3.** 2,4,6,8,9,10,12,14 **4.** 1,2,3,5,7,11,13,17,19 **5a.** 1,2,3,4,6 and 12 **b.** 1,2,4,8 and 16 **c.** 1,2,3,6,9 and 18 **6a.** **b.** **c.**

Number Patterns: 1a. 83.85, 8.385, 0.8385 **b.** 32,128,512 **c.** 565, 715, 865 **d.** 648, 612, 576 **e.** 200, 2000, 20000 **2.** 6, 12, 18, 24, 36, 42, 48, 54, 60, 66, 72, 78, 84, 90, 96 **3.** 1, 3, 10, 15, 21, 28, 36 **4.** 4, 9, 16, 25, 36, 49, 64 **5a.** 25 **b.** 64 **c.** 49 **d.** 100 - square number **6a.** 4 **b.** 36 **c.** 81 **d.** 49 **e.** 9 **f.** 2

Angles: 1a. Teacher/Parent reflex **b.** Teacher/Parent right angle **c.** Teacher/Parent obtuse **2a.** Parent/Teacher **3a.** 30° **b.** 110° **c.** 90° **d.** 70° **e.** 47° **f.** 35° **4a.** 300° **b.** 230° **c.** 275° **5a.** 180° **b.** 360° **6.** 3

Circles: 1a. Diameter **b.** sector **c.** arc **d.** semicircle **e.** chord **f.** circumference **g.** radius **h.** quadrant **2a.** 5cm **b.** 8cm **c.** 7cm **3a.** semicircle **b.** arc **c.** centre **d.** 18cm **e.** centre **4.** Teacher/Parent

Unit 16

Money: 1a. $9 **b.** $1.20 **c.** $3.24 **d.** $4.80 **e.** $3.75 **f.** $4.55 **2a.** 30% **b.** 50% **c.** 60% **d.** 20% **e.** 75% **f.** 10% **g.** 25% **h.** 30% **i.** 80% **3a.** $10 **b.** $2 **c.** $50 **d.** $20 **e.** $75 **f.** $15 **4a.** $10 **b.** $20 **c.** $6 **d.** $14 **5a.** $ 150 **b.** $3

Fractions: 1. Parent/Teacher **a.** **b.** **c.** **d.** **e.** **f.** **2a.** 2/8 **b.** 6/8 **c.** 4/10 **d.** 9/12 **e.** 4/6 **f.** 8/10 **3a.** 4/6 + 1/6 = 5/6 **b.** 5/8 + 2/8 = 7/8 **c.** 3/10 + 4/10 = 7/10 **c.** 3/10 + 4/10 = 7/10 **d.** 4/6 - 1/6 = 3/6 **e.** 7/8 - 6/8 = 1/8 **f.** 7/10 - 4/10 = 3/10 **4a.** 4/4 - 1/4 = 3/4 **b.** 5/5 - 2/5 = 3/5 **c.** 8/8 - 3/8 = 5/8

Transformation: 1a. **b.** ∞ **c.** ✚ **2a.** **b.** W **c.** X **d.** 8 **3a.** Translate (slide) **b.** rotate **c.** reflect **d.** rotate **4.** Teacher - patterns will vary.

Chance: 1. Parent/Teacher a-d answers will vary **2a.** 10% **b.** 20% **c.** 20% **d.** 0% **e.** 40% **3a.** 50% **b.** 25% **c.** 1/13 **d.** Parent/teacher **e.** Parent/teacher

Unit 17

Ordering of Operations: 1a. 10 **b.** 45 **c.** 8 **d.** 12 **e.** 2 **f.** 4 **g.** 25 **h.** 5 **2a.** 25 **b.** 4 **c.** 5 **d.** 7 **e.** 3 **f.** 11 **g.** 9 **h.** 11 **3a.** 8 **b.** 27 **c.** 11 **d.** 3 **e.** 6 **f.** 5 **g.** 29 **h.** 5 **4a.** 5 **b.** 4 **c.** 4 **d.** 7 **e.** 4 **f.** 24 **5a.** 24 **b.** 120 **c.** 60

Decimal Fractions: 1a. 1/4 **b.** 3/4 **c.** 7/10 **d.** 1/2 **e.** 1/8 **f.** 2/5 **g.** 2/3 **h.** 1/5 **i.** 4/5 **j.** 1/3 **k.** 7/8 **l.** 3/5 **2a.** tenths **b.** ones **c.** hundredths **d.** tenths **e.** tens **f.** thousandths

Answers

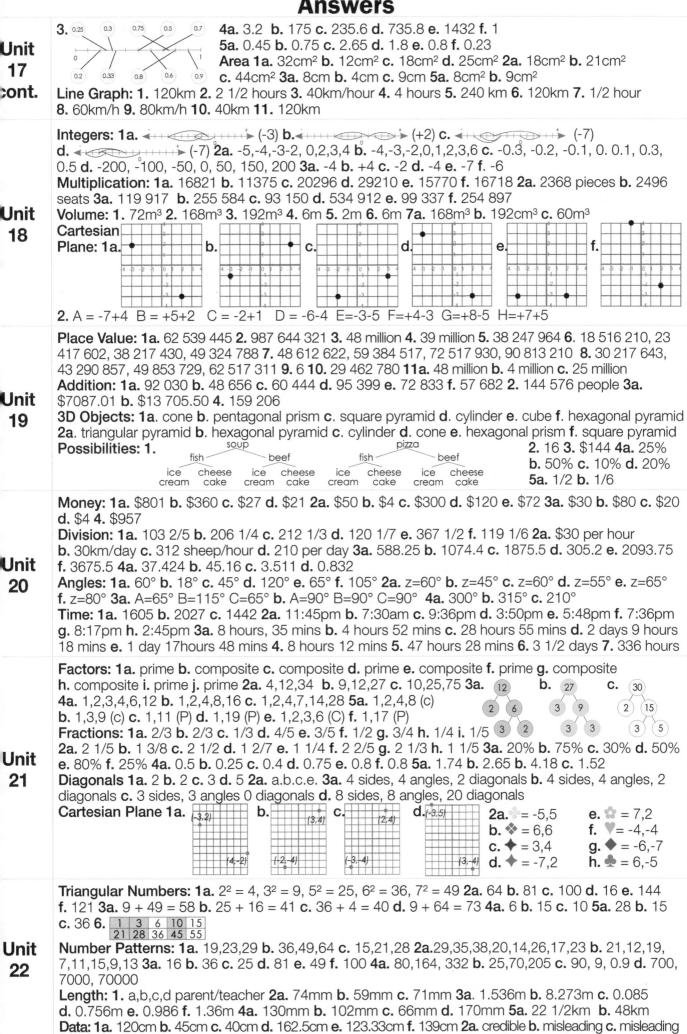

Unit 17 cont.

3. [number line with fractions matched: 0.25, 0.3, 0.75, 0.5, 0.7 / 0.2, 0.33, 0.8, 0.6, 0.9]

4a. 3.2 **b.** 175 **c.** 235.6 **d.** 735.8 **e.** 1432 **f.** 1
5a. 0.45 **b.** 0.75 **c.** 2.65 **d.** 1.8 **e.** 0.8 **f.** 0.23
Area 1a. 32cm² **b.** 12cm² **c.** 18cm² **d.** 25cm² **2a.** 18cm² **b.** 21cm²
c. 44cm² **3a.** 8cm **b.** 4cm **c.** 9cm **5a.** 8cm² **b.** 9cm²
Line Graph: 1. 120km **2.** 2 1/2 hours **3.** 40km/hour **4.** 4 hours **5.** 240 km **6.** 120km **7.** 1/2 hour
8. 60km/h **9.** 80km/h **10.** 40km **11.** 120km

Unit 18

Integers: 1a. [number line] (-3) **b.** [number line] (+2) **c.** [number line] (-7)
d. [number line] (-7) **2a.** -5,-4,-3-2, 0,2,3,4 **b.** -4,-3,-2,0,1,2,3,6 **c.** -0.3, -0.2, -0.1, 0. 0.1, 0.3,
0.5 **d.** -200, -100, -50, 0, 50, 150, 200 **3a.** -4 **b.** +4 **c.** -2 **d.** -4 **e.** -7 **f.** -6
Multiplication: 1a. 16821 **b.** 11375 **c.** 20296 **d.** 29210 **e.** 15770 **f.** 16718 **2a.** 2368 pieces **b.** 2496
seats **3a.** 119 917 **b.** 255 584 **c.** 93 150 **d.** 534 912 **e.** 99 337 **f.** 254 897
Volume: 1. 72m³ **2.** 168m³ **3.** 192m³ **4.** 6m **5.** 2m **6.** 6m **7a.** 168m³ **b.** 192cm³ **c.** 60m³
Cartesian Plane: 1a. **b.** **c.** **d.** **e.** **f.** [six Cartesian plane graphs]
2. A = -7+4 B = +5+2 C = -2+1 D = -6-4 E=-3-5 F=+4-3 G=+8-5 H=+7+5

Unit 19

Place Value: 1a. 62 539 445 **2.** 987 644 321 **3.** 48 million **4.** 39 million **5.** 38 247 964 **6.** 18 516 210, 23
417 602, 38 217 430, 49 324 788 **7.** 48 612 622, 59 384 517, 72 517 930, 90 813 210 **8.** 30 217 643,
43 290 857, 49 853 729, 62 517 311 **9.** 6 **10.** 29 462 780 **11a.** 48 million **b.** 4 million **c.** 25 million
Addition: 1a. 92 030 **b.** 48 656 **c.** 60 444 **d.** 95 399 **e.** 72 833 **f.** 57 682 **2.** 144 576 people **3a.**
$7087.01 **b.** $13 705.50 **4.** 159 206
3D Objects: 1a. cone **b.** pentagonal prism **c.** square pyramid **d.** cylinder **e.** cube **f.** hexagonal pyramid
2a. triangular pyramid **b.** hexagonal pyramid **c.** cylinder **d.** cone **e.** hexagonal prism **f.** square pyramid
Possibilities: 1. [tree diagram: soup/pizza → fish/beef → ice cream/cheese cake]
2. 16 **3.** $144 **4a.** 25%
b. 50% **c.** 10% **d.** 20%
5a. 1/2 **b.** 1/6

Unit 20

Money: 1a. $801 **b.** $360 **c.** $27 **d.** $21 **2a.** $50 **b.** $4 **c.** $300 **d.** $120 **e.** $72 **3a.** $30 **b.** $80 **c.** $20
d. $4 **4.** $957
Division: 1a. 103 2/5 **b.** 206 1/4 **c.** 212 1/3 **d.** 120 1/7 **e.** 367 1/2 **f.** 119 1/6 **2a.** $30 per hour
b. 30km/day **c.** 312 sheep/hour **d.** 210 per day **3a.** 588.25 **b.** 1074.4 **c.** 1875.5 **d.** 305.2 **e.** 2093.75
f. 3675.5 **4a.** 37.424 **b.** 45.16 **c.** 3.511 **d.** 0.832
Angles: 1a. 60° **b.** 18° **c.** 45° **d.** 120° **e.** 65° **f.** 105° **2a.** z=60° **b.** z=45° **c.** z=60° **d.** z=55° **e.** z=65°
f. z=80° **3a.** A=65° B=115° C=65° **b.** A=90° B=90° C=90° **4a.** 300° **b.** 315° **c.** 210°
Time: 1a. 1605 **b.** 2027 **c.** 1442 **2a.** 11:45pm **b.** 7:30am **c.** 9:36pm **d.** 3:50pm **e.** 5:48pm **f.** 7:36pm
g. 8:17pm **h.** 2:45pm **3a.** 8 hours, 35 mins **b.** 4 hours 52 mins **c.** 28 hours 55 mins **d.** 2 days 9 hours
18 mins **e.** 1 day 17hours 48 mins **4.** 8 hours 12 mins **5.** 47 hours 28 mins **6.** 3 1/2 days **7.** 336 hours

Unit 21

Factors: 1a. prime **b.** composite **c.** composite **d.** prime **e.** composite **f.** prime **g.** composite
h. composite **i.** prime **j.** prime **2a.** 4,12,34 **b.** 9,12,27 **c.** 10,25,75 **3a.** [factor tree 12] **b.** [factor tree 27] **c.** [factor tree 30]
4a. 1,2,3,4,6,12 **b.** 1,2,4,8,16 **c.** 1,2,4,7,14,28 **5a.** 1,2,4,8 (c)
b. 1,3,9 (c) **c.** 1,11 (P) **d.** 1,19 (P) **e.** 1,2,3,6 (C) **f.** 1,17 (P)
Fractions: 1a. 2/3 **b.** 2/3 **c.** 1/3 **d.** 4/5 **e.** 3/5 **f.** 1/2 **g.** 3/4 **h.** 1/4 **i.** 1/5
2a. 2 1/5 **b.** 1 3/8 **c.** 2 1/2 **d.** 1 2/7 **e.** 1 1/4 **f.** 2 2/5 **g.** 2 1/3 **h.** 1 1/5 **3a.** 20% **b.** 75% **c.** 30% **d.** 50%
e. 80% **f.** 25% **4a.** 0.5 **b.** 0.25 **c.** 0.4 **d.** 0.75 **e.** 0.8 **f.** 0.8 **5a.** 1.74 **b.** 2.65 **b.** 4.18 **c.** 1.52
Diagonals 1a. 2 **b.** 2 **c.** 3 **d.** 5 **2a.** a.b.c.e. **3a.** 4 sides, 4 angles, 2 diagonals **b.** 4 sides, 4 angles, 2
diagonals **c.** 3 sides, 3 angles 0 diagonals **d.** 8 sides, 8 angles, 20 diagonals
Cartesian Plane 1a. [graph (-3,2)/(4,-2)] **b.** [graph (3,4)/(-2,-4)] **c.** [graph (2,4)/(-3,-4)] **d.** [graph (-3,5)/(3,-4)]
2a. ✿ = -5,5 **e.** ✿ = 7,2
b. ✾ = 6,6 **f.** ♥ = -4,-4
c. ✦ = 3,4 **g.** ◆ = -6,-7
d. ✦ = -7,2 **h.** ♣ = 6,-5

Unit 22

Triangular Numbers: 1a. 2² = 4, 3² = 9, 5² = 25, 6² = 36, 7² = 49 **2a.** 64 **b.** 81 **c.** 100 **d.** 16 **e.** 144
f. 121 **3a.** 9 + 49 = 58 **b.** 25 + 16 = 41 **c.** 36 + 4 = 40 **d.** 9 + 64 = 73 **4a.** 6 **b.** 15 **c.** 10 **5a.** 28 **b.** 15
c. 36 **6.**

1	3	6	10	15
21	28	36	45	55

Number Patterns: 1a. 19,23,29 **b.** 36,49,64 **c.** 15,21,28 **2a.** 29,35,38,20,14,26,17,23 **b.** 21,12,19,
7,11,15,9,13 **3a.** 16 **b.** 36 **c.** 25 **d.** 81 **e.** 49 **f.** 100 **4a.** 80,164, 332 **b.** 25,70,205 **c.** 90, 9, 0.9 **d.** 700,
7000, 70000
Length: 1. a,b,c,d parent/teacher **2a.** 74mm **b.** 59mm **c.** 71mm **3a.** 1.536m **b.** 8.273m **c.** 0.085
d. 0.756m **e.** 0.986 **f.** 1.36m **4a.** 130mm **b.** 102mm **c.** 66mm **d.** 170mm **5a.** 22 1/2km **b.** 48km
Data: 1a. 120cm **b.** 45cm **c.** 40cm **d.** 162.5cm **e.** 123.33cm **f.** 139cm **2a.** credible **b.** misleading **c.** misleading

Answers

Unit 23

Decimal Fractions: 1. 0.9 **2.** 328.8 **3.** False **4.** 87% **5.** hundredths **6.** 7 **7.** 0.6 **8.** 0.35 **9.** 75% **10.** $160 **11a.** 0.32 **b.** 0.74 **c.** 3.72 **d.** 0.107 **e.** 70.45 **f.** 2.02 **12a.** 1/5 **b.** 2/5 **c.** 1/2 **13a.** 0.25 **b.** 0.4 **c.** 0.7 **d.** 0.75 **e.** 0.5 **f.** 0.75 **14a.** 3/5 **b.** 1/8 **c.** 1/3 **d.** 7/8

Decimals: 1a. 101.36 **b.** 612.11 **c.** 836.45 **d.** 966.72 **e.** 738.86 **f.** 1086.65 **2a.** $5036 **b.** $9561.53 **c.** $6646.89 **d.** $7285.59 **3a.** 214.87 **b.** 229.08 **c.** 385.29 **4.** $20.88, change $139.12

Mass: 1 a,c,d,e **2a.** 3.655T **b.** 3.252T **c.** 2.587T **d.** 1.74T **e.** 0.785T **f.** 2.726T **g.** 0.075T **3a.** 6000kg **b.** 7500kg **c.** 3250kg **d.** 4750kg **e.** 2050kg **f.** 16000kg **4a.** 30kg **b.** 36kg **c.** 7g **d.** 300g **e.** 75g **f.** 3kg

Data/Time: 1a. 467km **b.** 504km **2a.** 110km/h **b.** 30km/h **c.** 90km/h **3a.** **b.** **4a.** 2 1/2 hours **b.** 180km **c.** 1/2 hour **d.** 390km

Unit 24

Averages: 1a. 1.68m **b.** 4kg **c.** 1.83m **2a.** 74.8 - NO **b.** 80km/h **3a.** 4463 **b.** 5.03 **c.** 54.89 **d.** 0.53 **e.** 1/

Improper Fractions 1a. 1 3/5 **b.** 2 1/2 **c.** 1 2/3 **d.** 1 5/8 **e.** 1 3/4 **f.** 2 2/5 **g.** 3 2/3 **h.** 2 1/5 **i.** 2 2/3 **2a.** 14/8 = 1 3/4 **b.** 8/5 = 1 3/5 **c.** 12/8 = 1 1/2 **d.** 8/6 = 1 1/3 **e.** 6/5 = 1 1/5 **f.** 12/10 = 1 1/5 **3a.** 5/4 = 1 1/4 **b.** 11/8 = 1 3/8 **c.** 9/8 = 1 1/8 **d.** 13/8 = 1 5/8 **e.** 15/10 = 1 1/2 **f.** 13/10 = 1 3/10 **4a.** 3/2 **b.** 9/4 **c.** 7/4 **d.** 13/8 **e.** 9/2 **f.** 4/3

Volume Capacity: 1a. 500g/500cm³ **b.** 750g/750cm³ **c.** 2150g/2150cm³ **2a.** 3000L **b.** 390cm³ **c.** 250m **d.** 8m³ **e.** 960cm³ **f.** 400cm³ **3.** 250mL **4a.** 175mL mass 175g **b.** displacement 200mL mass 200g

Probability Combinations: 1. 0 - impossible, 0.25 unlikely, 0.5 - 50-50, 0.75 - possible, 1 - certain **2a.** 50-50 **b.** 0.25 **c.** 50-50. **d.** 1 **e.** 0 **3a.** 0 **b.** 50-50 **c.** 0 **d.** 1 **4a.** 4 **b.** 8

Unit 25

Money: 1a. $60 **b.** $75 **c.** $35 **d.** $200 **e.** $60 **f.** $180 **g.** $475 **h.** $620 **2a.** $64 **b.** $35.10 **c.** $45 **3a.** $240 **b.** $20475 **4a.** $21725 **b.** $83325 **5.** b,d,e

Multiplication: 1a. 3172 **b.** 4180 **c.** 2184 **d.** 4102 **e.** 2208 **f.** 992 **2a.** 85652 **b.** 197710 **c.** 34050 **d.** 196232 **e.** 165375 **f.** 191038 **3a.** $27872 **b.** 1778km **c.** 12760 seats

Angles: 1.a. 290° **b.** 245° **c.** 310° **d.** 100° **e.** 135° **f.** 55° **g.** X =45°, Y =135°, Z =45° **h.** X = 105°, Y = 75°, Z = 105° **i.** X = 50°, Y = 130°, Z = 50° **2a.** Z = 55° **b.** Z = 30° **c.** Z= 45° **3a.** z = 90° **b.** z = 65° **c.** z = 68° **d.** z = 120° **e.** 45° **f.** 85°

Locations: 1. **2a.** north-east **b.** east **c.** south east **d.** north **e.** south **f.** north-west **g.** west **h.** south-west **3a.** trapezium **b.** rhombus or parallelogram

Unit 26

Integers: 1a. - 1- 5 - 2 +12 = + 4 **b.** + 1 - 3 - 4 + 14 - 5 = 3 **c.** - 4 - 3 - 4 + 14 - 5 = - 2 **2.** ☆ 3,-3 ✿ 3,1 ❀ -2,4 ◆ 6,3 ♦ -5,-8 ✦ -4,8 ➚ -3,-5 ☺ -5,2 ✿ 2,-9 ✎ 4,7 ☎ 5,-7 **3a.** +5 **b.** -11 **c.** +8 **d.** +2 **e.** -10 **f.** -3 **g.** -8 **h.** -11

Fractions: 1a. 5/6 **b.** 7/10 **c.** 11/15 **d.** 7/12 **2a.** 5/4 = 1 1/4 **b.** 22/15 = 1 7/15 **c.** 27/20 = 1 7/20 **d.** 7/6 = 1 1/6 **3a.** 3/10 **b.** 5/12 **c.** 3/8 **d.** 5/12 **e.** 11/20 **f.** 1/6

Area: 1a. 8cm² **b.** 6cm² **c.** 13 1/2cm² **d.** 20cm² **2a.** 12cm² **b.** 32cm² **c.** 35cm² **d.** 27cm² **3a.** 3cm **b.** 4cm **c.** 4cm **4.** a,b,c, Parent/teacher

Graphs and Data: 1. **2a.** 140km **b.** 210km **c.** 4 1/2 hours **d.** 350km **e.** 7 hours **f.** 175km **3a.** 525km in total (extra 35km/70km/hour) **4.** 595km in total

Unit 27

Pascal's Triangle: 1a. 1,2,4,8,16,32,64,128 **2.** 1,3,6,10,15,21 **3a.** 1+3=4 **b.** 21+15=36 **c.** 3+6=9 **d.** 10+15=25 **e.** 6+10=16 **f.** 21+28=49 **4a.** 1,3,3,1 **b.** 1,5,10,10,5,1 **c.** 1,7,21,35,35,21,7,1 **5a.** 4 **b.** 16 **c.** 36 **d.** 25 **e.** 9 **f.** 49

Division: 1a. 3 **b.** 2 **c.** 14 **d.** 3 **e.** 3 **f.** 8 **g.** 8 **h.** 3 **2a.** 2567 1/2 **b.** 1535 3/4 **c.** 872 2/5 **d.** 713 7/10 **e.** 1291 1/4 **f.** 1254 3/5 **3a.** 1329.25 **b.** 1509.33 **c.** 764.2 **d.** 3208.5 **e.** 1193.143 **f.** 459.83 **4a.** 99 **b.** 155 **c.** 147 **d.** 129

Length: 1. 5km **2.** 6km **3.** 10mm **4.** approx 42 kilometres **5.** 17km **6.** 5cm **7.** 17km **8a.** 2.85km **b.** 7.2km **c.** 0.25km **d.** 0.42km **e.** 0.8km **f.** 1.75km

Time and Timetables: 1a. 8:37am **b.** 2349 **c.** 1220 **d.** 180km **2a.** 1:27pm **b.** 3:55pm **c.** 6:02pm **d.** 5:35pm **e.** 11:56pm **f.** 4:19pm **3a.** 1908 **b.** 1853 **c.** 2218 **d.** 1438 **e.** 1948 **f.** 2322 **4.** 1210

Unit 28

Place Value: 1a. 32 491 725 **b.** 27 549 071 **2.** thousand **3.** 87 643 210 **4.** 94 million **5a.** hundredths **b.** thousandths **c.** tenths **d.** tens **6a.** 62 333 124 **b.** 81 906 567 **c.** 12 245 616 **d.** 41 483 085

Fractions: a. 7/2 **b.** 7/4 **c.** 14/5 **d.** 17/4 **e.** 10/3 **f.** 17/10 **2a.** 5/12 **b.** 5/12 **c.** 3/10 **d.** 7/20 **e.** 3/10 **f.** 1/8 **3a.** 8/10 - 5/10 = 3/10 **b.** 9/12 - 4/12 = 5/12 **c.** 7/8 - 4/8 = 3/8 **d.** 8/12 - 3/12 = 5/12 **d.** 8/12 - 3/12 = 5/12 **4a.** 1 1/2 **b.** 1 3/4 **c.** 1 3/5 **d.** 3

Prisms and Pyramids: 1a. 1 face, 0 vertices, 1 edge **b.** 6 faces, 8 vertices, 12 edges **c.** 5 faces, 6 vertices, 9 edges **d.** 7 faces, 7 vertices, 12 edges **e.** 10 faces, 16 vertices, 24 edges **f.** 5 faces, 5 vertices, 8 edges **g.** 6 faces, 8 vertices, 12 edges **h.** 4 faces, 4 vertices, 6 edges **i.** 6 faces, 6 vertices, 10 edges **2a.** front view and top view **b.** top view and side view **3a.** pentagonal prism **b.** square pyramid

Chance: 1a. 10% **b.** 25% **c.** 20% **d.** 50% **e.** 0% **f.** 100% **2a.** 1/2 **b.** 1/6 **c.** 1/4 **d.** 2/3 **e.** 0 none **3a.** 20% **b.** 6/10 = 3/5 **4.** a, b, parent/teacher **c.** maybe - probably not.